Berlitz

Jersey

Front cover: Gorey and Mont
Orgueil Castle

Right: the Archirondel Tower

TOP 10 ATTRACTIONS

Samarès Manor • A property renowned for its unique gardens and extensive range of plants *(page 46)*

Maritime Museum • A first-rate museum that brings to life Jersey's former seafaring role, ideal for adults and children *(page 34)*

Jersey Museum and Gallery • Provides an excellent introduction to the history and culture of the island *(page 29)*

Elizabeth Castle • On guard at the great Tudor stronghold, which was once occupied by Sir Walter Raleigh *(page 36)*

North Coast Footpath • The most exhilarating walk on the island, linking a chain of pretty bays such as Grève de Lecq *(pages 63 and 90)*

Jersey War Tunnels • An extraordinary complex of bomb-proof barracks constructed by the Germans *(page 38)*

La Hougue Bie • One of the largest and best-preserved Neolithic passage graves in Europe *(page 43)*

Beauport Beach • The islanders' favourite beach in a beautiful unspoilt bay *(page 55)*

Durrell Wildlife Conservation Trust • The renowned habitat for endangered species, in a delightful setting *(page 71)*

Mont Orgueil Castle • The stately symbol of the island dominates Gorey Harbour from its rocky promontory *(page 78)*

A PERFECT DAY

9.00am **Breakfast**

Indulge in a buffet breakfast in the Harbour Room of the Pomme d'Or Hotel in the heart of St Helier (Liberation Square; breakfast Mon-Sat from 7am–10am, Sun 8am–10am) and enjoy views of the yacht marina across the square.

12 noon **Heading north**

Explore at least a section of the majestic north coast, with its towering cliffs and perfect little fishing ports. Head north from Gorey via the B30 and B46, pass the famous Durrell Wildlife Conservation Trust, then dip down to quaint Bonne Nuit Bay, its tiny harbour sheltered by a single stone jetty.

12.45pm **Cliff walk**

Pick up the cliff footpath eastwards in the direction of Bouley Bay to see some of the North Coast's most spectacular scenery. For lunch try the seafood, crab sandwiches or Thai specials at Bonne Nuit's café, overlooking the pretty bay.

10.00am **Picture-postcard harbour**

Head out east from St Helier to Gorey, where the picture-postcard harbour sits below the great medieval stronghold of Mont Orgueil. Visit the Jersey Pottery at Gorey Village, stroll around the harbour and stop for coffee on the quayside.

IN JERSEY

3.30pm Afternoon relaxation

Relax on the beach here, take a dip or try your hand at wakeboarding or blokarting. If a quiet beach is more your scene, head a short distance west for the beautiful little bay of Beauport, reached down a bracken-covered cliff.

6.00pm Corbière

It's only a short hop to Corbière Lighthouse, Jersey's most dramatic landmark. Watch the sun dip into the Atlantic.

2.00pm St Aubin

Return to the south coast via the scenic Waterworks Valley and head east for St Aubin. Explore the port, browse in the Harbour Gallery arts and crafts centre, then head on west for St Brelade's Bay.

7.00pm Dinner options

Then enjoy gourmet fare at the Ocean Restaurant, Atlantic Hotel, with sublime views over St Ouen's Bay. (Advance booking, tel: 01534 744101). Cheaper options are pub grub with bay views at La Pulente, in St Ouen's Bay, or the seafood cafés along St Brelade's Bay.

10.00pm On the town

Back in St Helier spend a relaxing evening at the Royal Yacht Hotel, Weighbridge, right in the centre. Choose from bubbles in the POSH Champagne Bar or a nice quiet pint in the snug Cabin Bar. Alternatively just go with the flow in The Drift, a live music venue.

CONTENTS

41

77

13

Features

89

18

98

INTRODUCTION

Lying in the Bay of Mont St Michel, just 14 miles (22km) from the Normandy coast, Jersey has a distinct Gallic twist. The moment you arrive there is a sense of being abroad. Airport and harbour greet you with *Seyiz les bein-v'nus a Jèrri* (Welcome to Jersey) in the French Norman patois, street and place names are still written in French, islanders are known as *crapauds* (toads) and every restaurant has a *plateau de fruits de mer*. Yet Jersey feels reassuringly familiar to UK visitors. Although it's not truly British, it has been linked with the British Crown for over 900 years, the official language is English, you drive on the left and cash machines dispense sterling. In other words, Jersey has the best of both worlds.

Tilting southwards the island basks in the sun like a vast solar panel. The coastline offers a remarkable range of scenery from the vertiginous craggy cliffs of the north, to the Atlantic rollers of the windswept west, and the sweeping flat sands of the south. Along with its French flavour, the island offers all the ingredients of a traditional British seaside holiday: sandy beaches, crab-filled rock pools, big tides for beachcombing, picturesque fishing ports and ample family attractions. The Jersey sands are washed by clean blue seas and the island has one of the largest tidal movements in the world. Twice a day waters retreat to reveal large expanses of golden sands or lunar-like seascapes, pierced with rocks and

Plémont Bay on the North Coast

A doe-eyed Jersey cow

reefs. At low tide the island almost doubles in size – then the sea comes galloping in.

In the unlikely event you tire of the coast Jersey packs in plenty of other attractions. Its tempestuous history has left a mark in monuments ranging from Neolithic tombs to castles, coastal towers and wartime tunnels and bunkers. With walkers and cyclists in mind, Jersey has developed a network of Green Lanes where traffic is restricted to 15 mph (24kmph). Even on main roads the pace is slow, with a maximum speed limit of 40mph (64kmph). Inland Jersey is lush and pretty with wooded valleys, leafy lanes and pastures of doe-eyed cows.

But Jersey is no sleepy backwater. St Helier is a buzzing capital and haven of high finance; former grand hotels have been given multimillion facelifts, with swish spas added; forts and follies have been converted to stylish self-catering complexes; and beach resorts have seen a surge of adrenalin-fuelled sports in recent years. On the culinary scene Jersey has made quite a name for itself, with restaurants producing exceptional, freshly caught seafood. And the sedate speed limits don't deter the multimillionaires from driving around in plush Porches. Walking and cycling may be encouraged, but Jersey has one of the highest car ownership and user rates in the world.

'Peculiar of the Crown'
Neither wholly French nor English, Jersey has a quirky history and some unique, quasi-feudal customs. The Channel Islands

are termed a 'Peculiar of the Crown', pledging allegiance directly to the English Crown, not to the parliament of the UK. As the last remaining territories of the dukes of Normandy, they toast the Queen of England as 'Our Duke of Normandy'. They are not full members of the EU – though when Britain joined (the EEC) in 1973, the Channel Islands were granted special privileges. Jersey has its own government, legal system and even its own non-uniformed honorary police force who have operated since Norman times and who alone can formally charge a suspect. The island prints its own currency and still has a £1 note (which went out of circulation in the rest of Britain in the early 1980s); it also issues its own stamps.

Size and Climate

Minted in Jersey

Jersey may be the largest of the Channel Islands, but it is still a tiny island, measuring 9 miles (14km) long and 5 miles (8km) wide. Surprisingly it has a network of 350 miles (560km) of lanes giving it the feel of a much larger island. The most southerly of the British Isles, Jersey has more daily hours of sun than anywhere else in Britain. In summer the island has a daily average of eight hours of sunshine and an average maximum temperature of about 68°F (20°C). The best months to visit are from May to September, July and August being the hottest. Sea

Sandcastles at Ouaisné Bay

temperatures are chilly or refreshing, depending on your hardiness, averaging 62.8 °F (17.1°C) in summer.

The Bailiwick of Jersey embraces two offshore reefs: Les Minquiers, commonly known as the Minkies, 9 miles (14km) south of St Helier, and Les Ecréhous, 5 miles (8km) off the northeast coast. French adventurers occasionally attempt to take possession of the reefs and in 1950 the dispute over ownership was taken to the International Court in the Hague. The islands were awarded to Jersey – though French fishermen can still fish around the reefs.

Language

Until the Victorian era the common spoken language on the island was Jèrriais, a derivation of ancient Norman French. Large numbers of English settlers arrived on Jersey in the 19th century (many of them officers retired on half pay) and by the end of the century English was the prevalent language of St Helier. In all the country parishes, however, Jèrriais continued to be the main language until the 1960s. It is rarely heard these days but you might catch a few words from elderly locals in the countryside, perhaps at a market or agricultural auction. Only 3 percent of the population speak the patois fluently, but there has been a concerted effort to revive interest in the language. In 1999 the subject was brought into schools, and a GCSE is currently on the agenda. If you're on the island and interested in hearing the language tune in to BBC Radio Jersey 88.8FM/1026AM on Sunday morning at around 7.15am – or on alternate Fridays at 6.05pm. The *Jersey Evening Post* prints a daily proverb in Jèrriais, and has fortnightly articles with an English translation.

Jèrriais never enjoyed the status of standard French, or what was called *le bouôn français*. This was used in churches, law courts and administration and even today a few words are used for prayers before the States (or local government), court sittings and in official documents. Some street names in St Helier still have their original French names alongside the English ones given by 19th-century settlers from mainland Britain; eg, the somewhat prosaic Church Street was La Rue Trousse Cotillon – Pick Up Your Petticoat Street.

La Rocco Tower, constructed during the Napoleonic Wars

Economy

The economy saw major changes during the late 20th century as the financial services industry took over from agriculture and tourism as the mainstay of the economy. The sector is now completely dominant, accounting for more than half of the total economic activity in Jersey and employing over 25 per cent of the work force. The skyline of St Helier has seen a rash of high-rise HQs of banks, trusts, insurance and accountancy firms, along with apartment blocks for financial workers. According to the CIA *World Factbook*

2008, Jersey is the fourth richest country in the world based on GDP per capita. The Channel Islands have long attracted wealthy immigrants, seeking to benefit from the island's desirable lifestyle and advantageous tax laws. Only a handful are granted residency on Jersey each year through the High Value Residency initiative. Among the criteria is sufficient wealth to create tax for the Jersey States in excess of £100,000.

The tourist industry took off after World War II when sightseers arrived to see the relics of the German Occupation. The island's unique position as a holiday island close to France yet English speaking, with well-run hotels and guesthouses made it a holiday paradise from the 1950s. Tourism reached its peak in the late 1980s. Package holidays to Spanish costas and other cheaper destinations in the sun then led to a decline in tourism for the comparatively costly Channel Island. The industry also suffered as the finance service industry forged ahead in the 1990s and the island was no longer reliant on tourism, which currently accounts for a mere 3 percent of GDP. Over the last few years visitor numbers have steadily declined. By creating a new, younger image for the island, with emphases on active holidays, up-market short breaks, culture and gastronomy, Jersey Tourism is doing its best to lure them back.

St Aubin

A BRIEF HISTORY

It was around 6,500BC that Jersey became an island, cut off from the land mass of Europe by rising sea levels. Its vulnerable location led to a long and turbulent history. Striking reminders of its past are dotted all over the island, from the prehistoric burial grave at La Hougue Bie to coastal fortifications against the French, and the chilling Jersey War Tunnels from the German Occupation.

Little evidence was left by the earliest invaders but, from 1204, when King John lost Normandy to France and the Channel Islands chose to remain loyal to the English crown, successive defences were built against the invaders from France. The most recent fortifications date from the German Occupation in World War II when Hitler gave orders for the island to be transformed into 'an impregnable fortress'.

Prehistory

The earliest inhabited site on the island – and one of Europe's most important prehistoric sites – is La Cotte de St Brelade, a cave south of Ouaisné Bay, first occupied a quarter of a million years ago in the Lower Palaeolithic age. This sheltered site was inhabited intermittently for the next 200,000 years, but only during the colder months when the sea level was low enough to walk across from what is now France. The piles of woolly mammoth and rhino bones that were discovered at the foot of the 98-ft (32-

Ancient relics

On rare occasions when the sands have been washed away by storms, you can see the remains of ancient tree stumps in St Ouen's Bay. These are the relics of an early Neolithic forest probably dating from the time when Jersey was linked to the continent.

m) cliff suggested that the cave-dwellers stampeded herds of animals over the cliff to their deaths. Archaeological investigations, which started here in 1881, and continued on and off until 1978, also brought to light 13 teeth belonging to a Neanderthal man or woman. The cave is closed to the public, but crucial relics are displayed in the Jersey Museum and the archaeological gallery at La Hougue Bie.

By 8000BC the climate was milder and Guernsey, Alderney and Sark had become islands. It was another two thousand years before Jersey broke away, and humans migrated here. Neolithic farmers established settlements from around 4000BC, clearing woodland and creating fields for crops and herds of sheep and cattle. The most conspicuous evidence of these settlers are the dolmens and menhirs scattered around the island. An outstanding example is the passage grave at La Hougue Bie (see page 43).

During the Bronze and Iron ages, the Channel Islands had trade links with Britain, Ireland and France. An outstanding example of an import from this era is the 5-ft (1.4-m) long gold torque discovered in St Helier in 1888, and on display

St Helier – Jersey's Patron Saint

Born to pagan parents in Tongeren in modern-day Belgium, the hermit Helerius is said to have brought Christianity to Jersey. He arrived on the island in the 6th century, and founded a hermitage in a cave on a tidal islet where Elizabeth Castle stands today. For 15 years he devoted his life to prayer and to the protection of the small settlement of fishermen. In AD555 Norman pirates landed on the islet, saw Helerius praying and cut off his head with axes –hence the two crossed axes on the emblem of St Helier. A monastery was founded here and Helerius was made a saint. His feast day is marked annually on the Sunday closest to July 16 by a pilgrimage to what is now known as Hermitage Rock.

Hermitage Rock, home of St Helier

at the Jersey Museum. From the Roman period a fair number of coins have been unearthed, but there is no concrete evidence of a Roman invasion.

The comparatively peaceful early Christian era was shattered by the Vikings who colonised Normandy. In 911 Rollo the Viking was made duke of Normandy on condition that he supported the king and protected the region from the invasions of other Vikings. The Duchy of Normandy expanded to the Channel Islands in 933 and the Normans made their mark with their feudal laws, seafaring traditions and language. An-oft quoted archaic Jersey law dating back to the Norman era is the right to invoke *La Clameur de Haro*, a cry for justice said to be created by Rollo. If a civilian feels his property is being threatened he may go down on bended knee in the presence of two witnesses, and cry: '*Haro! Haro! Haro! A l'aide, mon prince, on me fait tort*' (O Rollo! O Rollo! To my aid, my prince, I am being wronged'), followed by the

Annunciation fresco in the Fishermen's Chapel, St Brelade

Lord's Prayer in French. No further action or trespass can be taken until judgement is given in the appropriate court of law. The *Clameur* is rarely invoked today – the last time it was used successfully was in 1980. In 1994 a Jersey resident raised the *Clameur* against his brother in the Royal Square, but it was incorrectly invoked and therefore ignored. If the *Clameur* is used without justification the claimant is fined.

The British Connection

Following the victory of Norman Duke William II (William the Conqueror) at the Battle of Hastings, the Channel Islands became part of the Anglo-Norman realm. This was the beginning of the link with the English Crown, reinforced in 1204 when King John lost Normandy to France. The Channel Islands were given the choice of remaining loyal to the English Crown or reverting to France. They opted for the former, and in return the king granted them 'the continuance of their ancient laws and privileges', laying the foundation for self-government. Jersey was no longer a peaceful backwater – France, just across the water, became the foe.

The French Threat

Fear of invasion from France led to the construction of fortifications around the Jersey coast. In the early 13th century the great medieval fortress of Mont Orgueil was built to command the east coast, looking across to continental Normandy. 'Mount Pride' remained the chief stronghold of the island for nearly four centuries, but this was a bastion built for bows and arrows, and by the mid-16th century it was no longer up to defending the island. Work started on a new fortification on the islet of St Helier, built to withstand modern warfare and provide anchorage for the large merchant ships. Sir Walter Raleigh, who resided here as the island's governor, named it Fort Isabella Bellissima (Elizabeth the most Beautiful) in tribute to his beloved queen, Elizabeth I.

During the English Civil War, Jersey hoped to remain neutral, but local rivalries led to the island's own brief civil war. The island finally emerged on the side of the king, and provided shelter for members of the royal family. The young Prince of Wales took refuge here briefly in 1646, and following the execution of his father, King Charles I in 1649, came back and was proclaimed King Charles II by the Governor of Jersey, Sir George Carteret. As a reward, Charles II bequeathed to Carteret a large tract of land

States of Jersey

The States of Jersey, the island's parliament, first convened in the 16th century. Today it comprises the Lieutenant Governor, who is the Monarch's representative in the island, the Bailiff, the Dean of Jersey, the Attorney General and the Solicitor General – along with 12 senators, 12 parish constables and 29 deputies.

in the American colonies, henceforth known as New Jersey. Jersey's loyalty to the monarch led to an inevitable invasion force of Parliamentarians under Cromwell. In 1651, 80 vessels crossed to Jersey with more than 2,500 troops under Admiral Blake. Royalist resistance was crushed and Cromwell's new model army controlled the island.

Navigation and Knitting

Following the restoration of the monarchy Jersey enjoyed a phase of comparative peace and prosperity. Shipbuilders grew rich on cod-fishing in Newfoundland, splendid merchants' houses (known as 'Cod Houses') were constructed in St Aubin, while inland agriculture flourished. Cider was produced in large quantities and exported, sheep were abundant and the majority of the islanders (including men and children) were knitting stockings and fishermen's sweaters. (Legend has it that

Harvesting seaweed at Gorey Harbour

Mary Queen of Scots went to her execution wearing a pair of white Jersey stockings.) Knitting in fact became so popular and lucrative that the harvest crops and seaweed collection began to suffer. A new law was introduced in 1708 forbidding the making of stockings during harvest and vraicing (seaweed collecting). Islanders were made to work on the land 'on pain of imprisonment on bread and water and the confiscation of their work'.

Guide in period costume at St Helier's Elizabeth Castle

The Battle of Jersey

Jersey's privateering activities in the 1770s, when ships were licensed to plunder enemy vessels, led to two attempts by France to capture the island – first in 1779, and more famously, in 1781. On 6 January, under the command of Baron de Rullecourt, 600 troops took the island completely by surprise, landing at La Rocque in the southeast corner of the island and marching as far as Royal Square. The lieutenant-governor, still in bed, was tricked into believing that the enemy had around 14,000 troops, and immediately surrendered. However, the heroic Major Francis Peirson, a local 24-year-old officer, ignored the surrender and led the local militia to victory in the Battle of Jersey. Both Peirson and De Rullecourt were killed in action. This was the last attempt by France to capture the island. For fear of further invasions 30 Martello towers were constructed around the island, and many of these can still be seen today.

The Victorian Era

French vessels continued to be victims of Jersey privateers, leading to Napoleon's outcry: 'France can tolerate no longer this nest of brigands and assassins. Europe must be purged of this vermin. Jersey is England's shame'. With Napoleon's defeat at Waterloo, wars with France finally ceased. Although knitting and cider-making saw a decline, fishing, shipbuilding and agriculture still flourished. The prosperity of the island attracted newcomers, many of them army and navy officers retired on half pay after the Napoleonic Wars. By 1840 up to 5,000 English had settled here and by the end of the 19th century English had become the prevalent language of St Helier.

The German Occupation

The Channel Islands were the only British territory to fall into German hands during World War II. Tiny the islands may

Occupation Tapestry detail

have been but Hitler saw them as the first step to his intended invasion of the United Kingdom. In 1940 Churchill decided that the islands, which had no strategic value for Britain, could not justify the cost of defence and the decision was taken that they should be demilitarised. Prior to the arrival of Hitler's troops 90,000 people fled the island while 80,000 decided to stay. Within two years Jersey was turned into an impregnable fortress, with thousands of foreign forced

The German MP3 tower on the northwest coast

labourers and Russian prisoners-of-war toiling in harsh conditions to construct concrete walls, bunkers and gun emplacements. This was to be part of Hitler's Atlantic Wall project, a line of defence works extending all the way from the Baltic to the Spanish frontier. Over half a million tons of concrete were used around the coasts.

In the mistaken belief that an attack on the Channel Islands was imminent, Hitler gave orders for the construction of an emergency underground hospital for the treatment of German casualties – today's Jersey War Tunnels *(see page 38)*. Since the invasion never took place the hospital was never put to use. For the islanders the German Occupation was a time of hardship and deprivation, with shortages of food, fuel and medicines. During the last months the near-starving population was saved by the Swedish SS *Vega*, bringing Red Cross food parcels and other essential provisions. On 9 May 1945 British forces liberated the Channel Islands and the occupying forces surrendered peacefully. Citizens gathered to listen to Churchill's broadcast of the German capitulation 'And our dear Channel Islands are to be freed today'. Liberation Day on 9 May has been celebrated ever since.

Postwar Developments

After the war tourism was boosted by visitors from the UK, curious to see the after-effects of the Occupation. Tourism flourished up to the late 1980s, but since then numbers of holiday-makers have slowly declined. Meanwhile, stable government and advantageous tax laws led to the development of international financial services, including offshore banking, trust management and insurance. In the 1980s this took over as the main source of revenue for the island, and today more than 25 percent of the working population is employed in the financial services industry.

Jersey is not part of the United Kingdom but a dependency of the British Crown, as it has been since 1204, with the islanders owing their allegiance to the Queen. The island's parliament, known as the States of Jersey (see page 19), is responsible for running different sides of island life including Health, Education and Economic Development. Traditionally political parties have not played a major role on Jersey but changes to the ancient constitution came about with the introduction of ministerial government in 2005. The Jersey Democratic Alliance and the Centre Party were formed in 2005, followed by the Jersey Conservative Party in 2007.

A perfect day in St Brelade's Bay

Historical Landmarks

c.6000BC Jersey becomes an island when it is separated from the rest of Europe.

5000–2,850BC Neolithic Period. Megalithic tombs or dolmens are erected, including La Hougue Bie.

2,250–350BC Bronze and Iron ages.

6th century AD St Helier is martyred by pirates in 555.

933 Channel Islands annexed to the Duchy of Normandy.

1066 Battle of Hastings. Channel Islands become part of the Anglo-Norman realm.

1204 King John loses Normandy to France but the islands remain loyal to the English Crown and are granted self-government.

1204 Work starts on Mont Orgueil Castle.

1550–1600 Construction of Elizabeth Castle.

1642–51 English Civil War. After a brief period of civil war, Jersey emerges on the side of the Royalists.

1649 Charles I beheaded. Charles II (then Prince of Wales) takes refuge in Jersey and is proclaimed king by the governor.

1651 Parliamentarians sent to put down Royalist resistance.

1781 Battle of Jersey. The heroic Major Peirson leads the local militia to victory when the French attempt to take over the island.

1846 Queen Victoria visits Jersey.

1937 Jersey Airport opens.

1940 Channel Islands demilitarised; 10,000 evacuated from Jersey.

1940–4 German Occupation. Foreign prisoners brought to the island to build defences. Rationing introduced.

9 May 1945 Liberation of the Channel Islands.

1973 Britain joins the EEC (now the EU). Special terms are agreed for the Channel Islands.

2004 Jersey celebrates 800 years of allegiance to the Crown.

2005 The States of Jersey adopt modern ministerial government, replacing the antiquated committee system.

2009 Durrell Wildlife celebrates its 50th anniversary.

WHERE TO GO

Jersey is a tiny island of 9 miles (14km) by 5 miles (8km), but the network of 350 miles (560km) of roads, many of them narrow lanes, plus the speed limit of 40 mph (64km/h) and even 15 mph (24km/h) on some rural roads gives the impression it's far bigger. The island is divided up into 12 parishes – not that you would be aware which one you were in when driving around the island. Each parish has its own stretch of coastline, and wherever you are based on the island you are never far from a good beach.

The land slopes from the dramatic cliffs on the north coast to the flat sandy beaches of the south. The capital and hub of the island is St Helier on the south coast, which is the best centre for shopping and bus transport to attractions and beaches. However, you may prefer smaller, prettier and less traffic-thronged resorts such as Gorey or St Aubin – or the beach resort of St Brelade. If you don't have your own car these three centres all have good bus connections.

The following pages start with St Helier and then take in some inland excursion destinations from the capital before going around the coast in a clockwise direction. Travelling from the south to north or north to south, often via picturesque valleys, is another option – but travelling east to west or vice versa is trickier unless you know the island well.

ST HELIER

Capital of Jersey and its only real town, **St Helier** took its name from the hermit, Helerius, who arrived here in the 6th century *(see page 16)*. It was not until the 19th century that

Mont Orgueil Castle and Gorey Harbour

Jersey Museum and Gallery

St Helier was developed as a main town with its harbours extended to become a commercial port. Today the first impressions are hardly picturesque. Arriving by sea you are greeted by a power station, cranes, high-rise blocks and traffic-thronged streets. However, the centre of the capital reveals a more charming side with its markets, museums and pedestrianised streets. **Jersey Tourism**, where you can pick up all sorts of useful information, is on Liberation Place, just along the Esplanade from Liberation Square.

Liberation Square

A ▶ It was in **Liberation Square** that crowds of islanders gathered on 9 May 1945 to welcome the British fleet that had come to release them after five gruelling years of German Occupation. The **Liberation Sculpture**, representing islanders and a British soldier clutching the Union Jack, was placed here in 1995, the fiftieth anniversary of the Liberation. The Union Jack which featured in the original sculpture was then changed to a group of doves by the Occupation and Liberation Committee. Following comments about islanders being more likely to eat the doves than release them (food shortages were severe during the Occupation) the Union Jack was reinstated. On the north side of the square the **Pomme d'Or Hotel** overlooking the harbour provided a prime site for the German

Naval Headquarters during the Occupation. On Liberation Day, in front of crowds of islanders, the Union Jack was raised on the balcony of the building, replacing the swastika.

Jersey Museum and Gallery

Just east of Liberation Square, the **Jersey Museum and Gallery** (daily 9.30am–5pm; charge; www.jerseyheritage.org) offers an excellent introduction to the island, tracing its story from prehistoric to present times. This fine town house, which once stood on the seafront, was built for a wealthy shipowner in 1818 and the upper floors have been faithfully reconstructed as a Victorian merchant's house. On the ground floor you can see some fascinating archive footage on the island, and a reconstruction of a paleolithic cave scene at La Cotte de St Brelade, where cave dwellers hunted animals by stampeding them off the clifftops. The first floor is devoted to the

The Jersey Lily

Two portraits of Jersey's most famous daughter, Lillie Langtry (1853–1929) herald the second-floor art gallery. Born Emilie Charlotte Le Breton, daughter of a dean of Jersey, she married a wealthy widower, Edward Langtry, at the age of 21. They moved to London where she led the field in fashion and, on becoming the semi-official mistress of the Prince of Wales (later King Edward VII), the talk of the town. The portraits by Sir John Everett Millais, also a Jersey native, and Sir Edward Poynter, were both crowd-pullers at the Royal Academy in 1878 – a year after she had become the Prince of Wales' mistress. Lillie went on to become a highly successful actress – the first society woman to go on the stage. She took up American citizenship in 1897, divorced her husband, remarried and bought a ranch in California. She died in Monte Carlo and is buried in the graveyard in the church of St Saviour with the rest of her family.

story of Jersey, and its culture and traditions, including oyster-catching, shipbuilding, farming, knitting and tourism.

Parish Church of St Helier

C Just north of Jersey Museum the **Parish Church of St Helier** was a nerve centre of the town in times gone by. A church has stood here since the 11th century and it was a place where locals sought refuge in times of crisis, elections were held and bells were rung when enemy ships were sighted. Below the pulpit a memorial is dedicated to the heroic Major Peirson, who was killed in nearby Royal Square in the Battle of Jersey; his enemy, the Baron de Rullecourt, has a stone memorial in the graveyard. On the far side of the churchyard, Church Street still retains its fetching French-Norman name alongside the English. La Rue Trousse Cotillon or 'Pick Up Your Petticoat Street' dates from the times when ladies had to lift up their dresses to avoid mud, drains and sewers. The street leads into Library Place, where the aptly named Constable of St Helier, Pierre le Sueur, who founded the underground sewage system, is honoured with an obelisk.

Statue of George II in Royal Square

Royal Square

East of Church Street the peaceful, leafy **Royal Square** **D** was formerly the hub of town life. This used to be the marketplace, and it was here that proclamations were announced, prisoners awaited trial in a wooden cage and petty offenders were flogged or put in the pillory or stocks. In 1648 two witches were strangled and burnt at the stake in the square. Happier events take place these days, such as weddings (for UK as well as Jersey residents) in the former corn market. In the centre of the square a stone commemorates the Battle of Jersey *(see page 21)* which took place here in 1871. The conspicuous gilded statue is King George II (1727–60), dressed as Caesar – but wearing the Order of the Garter. He was given this place of honour after donating £300 for the construction of St Helier's first harbour and the square's name was changed from the Market Place to Royal Square.

Al fresco at the Peirson pub on Royal Square

The king's coat of arms can be seen above the entrance of the **Royal Court**, the island's court of justice, on the south side of the square. On 8 May 1945 the bailiff of Jersey stood on the balcony here in front of a seething mass of islanders and relayed Churchill's message that the Channel Islands were to be freed. The **States Chamber**, Jersey's Parliament, stands to the left of the Royal Court. Visitors to the public gallery are welcome and there are guided tours on Saturday morning. (Access is from Halkett Place, where you can normally view the Order Paper for the day.)

If you look carefully at the paving stones in the west half of the square you will see a large 'V' for Victory, which was secretly inscribed by a local stonemason while relaying the flagstones during the latter stages of the Occupation. Discovery of such acts of subversion would often lead to deportation, and he hid the 'V' under a layer of sand. The letters 'EGA' and '1945' were later added to commemorate the arrival of the Swedish Red Cross Ship, SS *Vega*. Both occupiers and islanders by this stage were near starvation but it was only civilians who were allowed the parcels from the ship. The Germans just watched as excited local people ripped opened their packets of cheese, chocolate and dried eggs.

Shopping Streets and Markets

From Peirson Place beside the pub you can access **King Street**, which, with **Queen Street**, makes up the main pedestrianised shopping thoroughfare. As well as the usual High Street chain stores there are individual retail outlets, including a remarkable number of jewellers. At Charing

Inside the Central Market

Cross at the western end a large metal *crapaud* (the symbolic Jersey toad) sits atop a granite pillar. The sculpture marks the site of an 18th-century prison and is engraved with the crimes and punishments of the time. At the other end of the street turn right for Halkett Place and the **Central Market** ◄ⓔ (Mon–Wed, Fri–Sat 7.30am–5.30pm, Thur 7.30am–2pm) on the other side of the street. A wonderful array of fresh produce – strawberries, asparagus, Jersey herbs and home-grown flowers – is laid out in this splendid Victorian glass-roofed building. The central feature is an ornate three-tiered fountain where cherubic figures lean on water jars with their paddles and gold-fish swim in the pool below. Apart from fruit and vegetable stalls there are butchers and bakeries, a delicatessen and a dairy shop with products from the famous Jersey cow. La Mare Jersey specialities are sold at Spice House: *nier beurre* or black butter *(see page 105)*, plus jams, jellies, wine and liqueurs.

For the **Fish Market** (also known as Beresford Market, same hours as Central Market) exit Central Market on the far side and turn left for Beresford Street. The building is modern without the elegance of Central Market, but there's a great spread of fresh fish, both local and imported. From Jersey waters you can expect to find live lobster, spider- and

Kingdom of Congers

The firm oily meat of the conger eel was regarded as a delicacy, and it used to be salted, dried and preserved throughout the winter. The conger-rich waters and the popularity of the eel led to the island's nickname in the 17th century: the Kingdom of Congers. The eel was sold to the wealthy, while the poor fishermen were left with the bony head. This, however, was the key ingredient for a flavoursome fish soup, traditionally garnished with marigold petals.

chancre crabs, scallops, prawns, locally farmed oysters and mussels, and amongst the fish, conger eel, wrasse and grey mullet. If all this looks tempting and it's time for a break, try out one of the two eateries here for a fishy snack and glass of wine.

At the end of Beresford Street you'll come face to face with a group of life-sized bronze Jersey cattle, including a calf looking suspiciously at a tiny *crapaud* or toad (the island mascot). Just to the north the **Jersey Arts Centre** is a lively venue that hosts regular exhibitions of contemporary art, as well as concerts and theatre productions.

Along the Waterfront

On North Quay, across the busy A1 from Liberation Square, the **Maritime Museum** (daily 9.30am–5pm; charge; www. jerseyheritage.org) occupies a 19th-century warehouse. This first-rate museum brings to life Jersey's former role as a seafaring state. It is very much an interactive museum where you can feel the force of the sea, learn how to design and sail a ship, tie a sheepshank and listen to songs and stories of the sea. Among the highlights are a full-size replica of the bow of the Jersey built brig, the *Orient Star*, and the Voyage Globe, a giant animatronic globe illustrating the journeys of Jersey's ships all over the world. On three days a week you can watch volunteer boat builders repair and maintain the museum's fleet of historic vessels. Examples of the restored boats can sometimes be seen in the marina outside the museum.

The museum shares the building with the **Occupation Tapestry Gallery** (same opening hours and same entrance ticket as the Maritime Museum). The 12 richly coloured tapestries depict scenes of the German Occupation, from the announcement of war, through deprivation and deportation to the arrival of Red Cross parcels and Liberation. These finely worked panels were designed and stitched by the islanders to

Detail of the Steam Clock

commemorate the 50th anniversary of Liberation, with each of the 12 parishes submitting a tapestry.

Next to the museum on the east side you are unlikely to miss the world's largest **Steam Clock**, modelled on a 19th-century paddle steamer. The benches here and around the old harbour basin record local vessels and their builders. Some of the ships sailed the oceans of the world, others worked the North Atlantic and the triangular trading routes based on the cod-fisheries, while the smaller vessels plied their trade in home waters.

The Waterfront Centre

The whole waterside area to the west is known as **The Waterfront Centre**. After years of political wrangling, this development is only half complete, and what has gone up so far has been hugely controversial. This vast space by the sea, with so much potential, and intended as 'the new maritime

La Frégate, a distinctive
waterfront café

quarter reconnecting the town with the seashore', intended to 'breathe new life into the town and the island, enriching the quality of life of resident and visitor alike' has been ruined by utilitarian high-rise buildings, car parks, and a huge carbuncle of a hotel right on the water's edge. Most tourists give the area a wide berth – and certainly no one comes here for a seaside stroll. The main attractions, aimed more at young local residents than visitors, are a leisure centre, multiplex cinema, and a couple of nightclubs and fast-food outlets. At the northern end **Les Jardins de la Mer**, gardens with a fountain, brings some light relief, and the terrace of the **Frégate Café** provides fine views of Elizabeth Castle.

Elizabeth Castle

Guarding the entrance of St Helier harbour, lies the great Tudor stronghold of **Elizabeth Castle** (early Apr–Oct 10am–6pm, last admission 5pm; charge; www.jerseyheritage. com), which defended the island for over 300 years. On an islet in St Aubin's Bay, the castle is connected to the shore by a causeway which you can cross at low tide. When the water is up the only means of access is the amphibious blue Castle Ferry which leaves at all tides from West Park slip (near Les Jardin de la Mer) and makes an enjoyable trip on a fine day.

By the late 16th century the great Mont Orgueil on Jersey's east coast was becoming increasingly vulnerable and a new fortification was required to meet the demands of modern-day warfare. Queen Elizabeth I ordered its construction and Sir Walter Raleigh, who lived here as governor, named it Fort Isabella Bellissima (Elizabeth the Most Beautiful) after his queen. The fortification was expanded several times in the 17th century, though this didn't prevent it coming under fire from mortars during the English Civil War. Philip Carteret, the then-governor, sustained a siege here for 50 days and in 1651 a mortar shell attack by the Parliamentarians forced the Royalists to surrender. Charles II took refuge here on two occasions, once as Prince of Wales, and again, three years later, after the execution of his father, when he was proclaimed King Charles II. During World War II the Germans added to the fortification with bunkers, gun batteries and a command post at the top of the castle.

Visitors can explore the battlements and climb up to the oldest fortress of the Upper Ward where there are views of

Elizabeth Castle at high tide

Hermitage Rock. This was home of St Helier, Jersey's patron saint, for 15 years *(see page 16)*. Grassy banks, free-roaming chickens (and an oyster catcher who nests yearly beside the castle entrance) come as a pleasant surprise. Those visiting in the late morning are required to stand to attention as Gunner Gilman fires the noonday cannon and male visitors may be dragooned into marching the Parade Ground. Exhibitions cover the history of the garrison, the development of the cannon and the story of the Jersey Royal Militia.

Fort Regent

J ➤ The final fortress built on Jersey was **Fort Regent**, whose location is marked by the white spaceship-like dome on Mont de la Ville above the town. Fears of further French invasion led to its construction in 1806–14 but it was never needed to defend the island. The building was converted into a huge leisure centre in 1958. It used to be a great venue to take the family on a rainy day but the pool has been closed, sporting facilities have been reduced and, although concerts still take place in Gloucester Hall, the future of this wonderfully sited fort remains uncertain.

EXCURSIONS FROM ST HELIER

Jersey War Tunnels

Following the Führer's orders to turn the Channel Islands into 'an impregnable fortress', slave workers were put to work on creating command posts and gun emplacements around the island. The most evocative of all these German

2 ➤ fortifications is the **Jersey War Tunnels** (Les Charrières Malorey, St Lawrence; Feb–Nov daily 10am–6pm, last admission 4.30pm; charge; www. jerseywar tunnels.com), the vast underground complex of Ho8 (Höhlgangsanlage 8). By car, take the A1 west out of St Helier, turn right on to the A11

at Bel Royal, then follow the signs for the War Tunnels; they can also be accessed by bus No. 8a and the Island Explorer Red and Yellow routes.

Hundreds of forced labourers from all over Europe, including Russian and Polish prisoners-of-war, were used to create a complex of bomb-proof barracks to protect the garrison of around 12,000 men against assault from sea or air. The project involved 16 tunnels, requiring the excavation of thousands of tonnes of rock and 6,000 tonnes of concrete to line the tunnels. Work came to a halt in 1943 when news came through of an impending Allied invasion of Europe, and orders were given for the complex to be turned into a huge subterranean casualty clearing station. The wards, operating theatre and administrative rooms were to cater for hundreds of wounded. The allied landings never happened, the German forces surrendered peacefully on 9 May 1945 and the unused Ho8 was taken over by a British medical unit and virtually stripped of all its contents. A year later it opened to sightseers and souvenir-seekers.

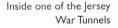

Inside one of the Jersey War Tunnels

Hospital scenes within the long, dark and chilly tunnels have been reconstructed, and a combination of archive film footage, islanders' reminiscences, photos and poignant

Garden of Reflection at the War Tunnels

correspondence chart life under the Nazis. The exhibits bring home the hardship endured by slave labourers (at least 560 died in the Channel Islands), the deprivation of islanders and the fate of those who were deported to camps in Germany. The site also incorporates the **Garden of Reflection**, designed for visitors to contemplate the suffering and deaths of the Occupation; and the **War Trail**, covering land once used as an artillery battery, and now being reclaimed by nature.

Jersey's Living Legend Village

Set in 8½ acres (3.5 hectares) of countryside, **Jersey's Living Legend Village** (La Rue du Petit Aleval, St Peter; Apr–Oct daily 9.30am–5pm, Mar and Nov Sat–Wed 9.30am–5pm; grounds free, separate charges for the Jersey Experience, Adventure Golf and Karting; www.jerseyslivinglegend.co.je) is a purpose-built attraction incorporating a multisensory history of Jersey, two 18-hole adventure golf courses set among caves, lakes and waterfalls and a Formula 1-style karting complex. Add to this the adventure playground and indoor crèche, the craft and shopping village, musicians and mime artists in summer, and you should find something to keep the whole family entertained for at least half a day. It can be reached by taking the A1 west out of St Helier, turning right on to the A11 at Bel Royal, then following the signs for the Living Legend; Bus No. 8a and the Island Explorer Red Route will also get you there.

Within the village the **Jersey Experience** is a lively special effects show recreating the story of the island and featuring stars such as Brian Blessed (as St Helier) and Samantha Janus (as Lillie Langtry). Visitors start on the deck of a Victorian paddle steamer destined for St Helier, descend down the dark winding tunnel of time, encountering characters and creatures from local legends. The auditorium is a mock-up of the Manoir de la Brequette, a manor house lost beneath the sea centuries ago. The story starts with prehistoric Jersey and takes you right through to the German Occupation in World War II.

Hamptonne Country Life Museum

The 'goodwyf' at Hamptonne Country Life Museum

In the heart of rural Jersey is the **Hamptonne Country Life Museum** (La Rue de la Patente, St Lawrence; Apr–Oct daily 10am–5pm, last admission 4pm; www.jersey heritage.org; charge), which takes you back to farming life as it was three centuries ago. The most scenic route there is via **Waterworks Valley**: follow the A1 from St Helier until you are about half way round St Aubin's Bay, then turn inland at the C118. A refreshing antidote to frenetic St Helier, this is a peaceful green valley whose streams used to power six watermills. Today the island's main reservoirs are located here; beyond the Dannemarche Reservoir fork left on to the C119 for the museum. It can also be reached by bus Nos 7 and 7b.

A cluster of farm buildings has been faithfully restored and there are meadows, woodland and orchards to explore. Two houses have been recreated to demonstrate the living conditions of farming families in the 17th and 18th centuries. Expect a spinner, lacemaker or the 'Goodwyf' who will show you round or entertain you with local gossip from the ancient farming community. An exhibition is devoted to the Jersey cow, and another, entitled *The Camera Never Lies*, shows how Hamptonne acquired a new look as the fictional Wessex village of Mellstock for the 2005 ITV drama adaption of Thomas Hardy's *Under the Greenwood Tree*, starring Keeley Hawes. Children can meet Jersey calves, feed the chickens, explore the grounds and play in activity areas, inside and out. Hamptonne's café serves a range of Jersey specialities *(see page 104)* – or you can order a picnic to enjoy in the orchards or meadows (tel: 01534 863955 in advance).

A heavy-duty cider press

Orchid Foundation

Horticultural enthusiasts should not miss the **Eric** ◀ **5** **Young Orchid Foundation** (Victoria Village, Trinity; Wed–Sat 10am–4pm; charge) which displays an award-winning collection of orchids within a purpose-built nursery and exhibition complex. The late Eric Young first established his collection in Jersey in 1958 and within a decade it was recognised as one of the leading private collections in Europe. The complex features permanently planted landscapes that use raised beds, traditional Jersey granite, logs and branches, to show the orchids in all their splendour.

Award-winning orchids

The nursery is not a commercial outfit, but there are often a few orchids for sale.

La Hougue Bie

One of the largest and best preserved Neolithic passage graves in Europe, **La Hougue Bie** (La Route de la Hougue Bie, Grouville; Apr–Oct daily 10am–5pm, last admission 4pm; charge; www.jerseyheritage.org) has been a centre of activity for 6,000 years. To get there by car, take the A6 or A7 from St Helier to the Five Oaks roundabout, then turn right on to the B28 and follow the signs for La Hougue Bie. It is also served by bus route 3a and Island Explorer Green Route, and Jersey cycle routes 3 and 8. If on arrival you're wondering where the monument is, head for the huge grassy mound. This conceals a rubble cairn which was built on top of the dolmen and faced with dry-stone walling. Centuries later Christianity made its mark on the site by the construction of two little chapels on top of the mound.

Following the Reformation the site passed into private hands and Philippe d'Auvergne, the duke of Bouillon, converted the ruined chapels into a neo-Gothic folly that became known as The Prince's Tower. A hotel was added in the 19th century and the site became one of the island's first tourist attractions, complete with pleasure garden, bowling alleys and fine views. Excavations in 1924 necessitated the demolition of the hotel and tower and led to the discovery of a low passage leading to funeral chambers.

The roof height of the tunnel-like passage grave is only 5ft (1.4m) so you have to stoop to gain access to the funereal chamber. Built of huge blocks of stone topped by capstones, this dark, mysterious – and far from spacious – chamber would have been used for ritual and ceremonial functions, as well as for burials. Fragments of human and animal bones, along with flint arrowheads and pottery frag-

La Hougue Bie

ments, were discovered here during excavation. Limpet shells were found on top of the capstones; these could have had a religious significance – or they might have just been the leftovers from the dolmen builders' lunch.

A pathway leads up to the two restored chapels at the top of the mound. The **Chapel of Notre Dame de la Clarté** (Our Lady of the Dawn) was built in the late 12th century in alignment

Holy sepulchre

In the 1520s Dean Mabon, who had made a pilgrimage to the Holy Land, had a shrine built under the Jerusalem Chapel in imitation of the Holy Sepulchre in Jerusalem. According to a Protestant chronicler of the late 16th century, the dean claimed to receive visions of the Virgin Mary and staged fake miracles to encourage alms from pilgrims.

with the dolmen, suggesting that its Christian creators recognised the link between the ancient monument and the equinoctial alignment. In the 1520s Dean Mabon *(see panel)* added what became known as the **Jerusalem Chapel**, where, if you switch on the lights, you can see the faint outlines of two archangels.

During the Occupation in World War II a battalion command bunker was built on the Hougue Bie site, beside the burial mound. This now houses a memorial to the workers who were brought to the Channel Islands from Europe to work on the German fortifications. In one section the words of the slave labourers and their guards are recorded on metal plaques; in another the names of 503 victims are inscribed on a glass pillar.

Also on the site are galleries of geological and archaeological displays, highlights of which are animal remains from La Cotte de St Brelade *(see page 15)*, jadeite axe-heads that were traded across to Europe in 3000BC, and rare hordes of Iron and Bronze Age coins.

Samarès Manor and part of the extensive gardens

Samarès Manor

Fourteen acres (6 hectares) of gorgeous landscaped gardens are the highlight of **Samarès Manor** (Apr–Oct daily 9.30am–5pm; charge; www.samaresmanor.com) in St Clement's, southeast of St Helier (access either by car or bus Nos 1a and 18 or the Island Explorer Green Route).The grounds were originally designed in the 1920s by Sir James Knott, a shipping magnate and philanthropist, who spent the last 10 years of his life here. Knott's passion was plants from the East, hence the Japanese Garden, rock and water gardens and large ponds with islands and camellia plantations.

The gardens have undergone substantial restoration and redevelopment in recent years. The latest projects are the Exotics garden, the Hot Garden (Mediterranean style) and the trails through fields of wild flowers. Bordering the manor house is a delightful walled garden full of culinary, cosmetic and medicinal herbs. The former bring flavour to dishes served in the Herb Garden Café (also good for cream teas). Plants in the gardens with a red marker can be purchased and taken back to the UK. Samarès specialities are roses, herbs, hardy perennials and lavender – as well as favourites such as the Jersey agapanthus, ice plants and Echium (bee plants). Visitors can take a guided tour of the **Jersey Rural Life and Carriage Museum**, and from Monday to Saturday (extra charge) of the privately owned **manor house**. Children will probably prefer to meet the farm animals in the surrounding fields and paddocks.

THE SOUTHWEST

From St Helier a vast crescent of south-facing sands extends all the way to the picturesque port and resort of St Aubin's in the west. A headland with glorious bay views divides the port from St Brelade, where palm-fringed gardens overlook one of the finest beaches on the island. From here you can walk along the clifftops to the dramatically located Corbière Lighthouse. Cyclists, joggers or walkers can cover the southwestern corner of the island by following the route of the old Jersey Railway line. Opened in 1870 this ran from St Helier to St Aubin, following the bay, and was then extended to Corbière. The track was turned into a footpath after competition from buses led to the closure of the railway and in 1936 fire destroyed much of the rolling stock at St Aubin.

Portelet Bay viewed from Noirmont Point

Salted fish

At St Aubin, during spring tides, razor fish can be enticed from the sands by sprinkling salt on the key-hole shaped opening at the top of their burrow. They think it's the tide coming in.

St Aubin's Bay

Stretching from Elizabeth Castle to St Aubin, the bay is a long sweep of sheltered, unbroken sands. During spring tides the water laps the seawall, then retreats over 300m to expose the huge expanse of flat sands – so flat and expansive it was used for take-off and landings of De Havilland Dragons before Jersey's airport opened in 1937. St Aubin's is not the prettiest of the island's beaches, and it's a long trek through shallow waters for bathing, but the sea is normally calm and safe for children and water sports are plentiful.

Half way round the bay, on the A1 inland, St Matthew's Church at Millbrook is known as the **Glass Church** (Mon–Fri 9am–5pm, Sun service at 11am; free). The austere-looking church was built in 1840 but only attracted attention after the Parisian glass designer, René Lalique, embellished its interior in 1930s. He was commissioned by Lady Trent as a memorial to her husband, Jessie Boot, of Boots the Chemist. Panels, pillars, windows, the altar cross and the Art Deco angels are all rendered in opalescent glass, giving a soft glow to the church interior.

St Aubin

8 You wouldn't think it now but **St Aubin** was the island's commercial hub from the early 16th to the 18th centuries. Fishermen used to set off from here in small boats to cross the Atlantic in spring, returning in autumn with rich stocks of Newfoundland cod. The fish was dried and salted, then shipped to the Mediterranean and Central America, to be traded for wines, spirits and tobacco. Merchants who made fortunes from fishing and shipbuilding built grand four-storey houses (known as 'cod houses') along the shore or in steep narrow streets, some of which you can still see today.

Named after the 5th-century Bishop of Angers, protector against piracy, St Aubin ironically also acquired much of its wealth through profiteering during the English Civil War. Jersey was pro-Royalist and the local ships were licensed to capture boats belonging to the enemy. Booty from these attacks was stashed away in the Old Court House Inn overlooking the harbour, now a historic hotel and restaurant. The building may look familiar to *Bergerac* fans – it featured as The Royal Barge in the cops and robbers series back in the 1980s.

St Aubin today is a picturesque port, popular for its villagey atmosphere, seaside strolls and ample choice of quayside eateries. At low tide you can walk out to **St Aubin's**

St Aubin and its harbour

Fort (closed to the public), originally built in the 1640s to ward off French invaders and extended over the centuries. The last to leave their mark on the fort were the Germans during the World War II Occupation.

Noirmont and Portelet

A steep hill from St Aubin (A13) takes you through a wooded valley west towards St Brelade's Bay. Just after the hairpin bend you are unlikely to miss the **Shell Garden** (Mon–Sat 9.45am–4.45pm, Sun 9.45–11.45am, 2.30–4.45pm; charge), decorated with thousands of seashells. The next left turn brings you south to **Noirmont Point**, a windswept headland, once known as Niger Mons or Black Hill, after the dark clouds that gather here. Sitting on the clifftop is a huge German command bunker (Apr–Oct most Suns 11am–4pm) with a large observation tower. The well-preserved bunker is full of Occupation-related exhibits. Views from here encompass St Aubin's Bay and on a really clear day you can spot the coast of Brittany on the horizon.

To the west lies **Portelet Bay**, an inviting little beach with soft sands and a sheltered setting, accessed down a long flight of steps from the clifftop car park at the Old Portelet Inn. The offshore Ile au Guerdain, topped by a defensive tower, became known as Janvrin's

By the seaside at St Brelade's Bay

Tomb after an unhappy episode in its history. Janvrin was a sea captain who was refused landing at St Aubin's harbour when returning from plague-infested Nantes in Brittany in 1721. Janvrin then fell victim to the plague, and had to be buried on the island. His body was later transferred to St Brelade's cemetery.

Ouaisné and St Brelade's Bays

Portelet Common, west of Portelet Bay, is a 77-acre (31-hectare) nature reserve set on the clifftop, affording dramatic sea views across to St Brelade's Bay. Below the slopes on the north-facing side of the common lies La Cotte de St

Brelade (closed to the public), a major Palaeolithic site *(see page 15)*. To the west sea views stretch to the far end of St Brelade's Bay. Below is **Ouaisné** (prounounced 'Waynay') **Bay**, a spacious, sandy beach (accessed by a steep path from the common or by road) which is rarely crowded, even in midsummer. However the newly opened Beach House restaurant/café on the seafront, with fabulous views, is swelling out the numbers of visitors to the bay. Behind the beach the gorse-covered common is home to some rare species of fauna, including the Jersey green lizard, the agile frog and the Dartford warbler – though you would be lucky to spot them.

St Brelade's Bay lies beyond the rocky promontory and is accessed across the beach at low tide, or over the rocks when the water is up. This is justifiably Jersey's most popular beach resort: a large crescent of gently sloping, southern-facing sands, with clear blue waters and water sports galore. You can choose from blokarting (also called sand karting), kayaking, coasteering, bodyboarding, windsurfing, water-skiing,dinghy sailing, skim boarding and surfing. The newest addition is paddle surf, once practised by the beach boys of

Path to Freedom

The granite stairway from St Brelade's churchyard to the tiny harbour is one of the last remaining sections of a Perquage, or sanctuary path. In the pre-Reformation era criminals who sought refuge in a parish church and swore to leave the island and give away all their possessions could use one of the Perquage walks, which linked each parish church to the sea. From there they would take a boat and seek sanctuary in France. The Perquages ceased to exist in 1683 when King Charles II bequeathed them to Sir Edward de Carteret, Viscount of Jersey, who then sold the land to farmers who owned the neighbouring fields.

Waikiki. The sport involves standing on a surfboard and using a long-handled oar to propel yourself forward to catch the waves. Above the bay a boardwalk is flanked by cafés, restaurants and bucket-and-spade shops. Neat and colourful palm-lined gardens border the promenade while the slopes behind are dotted with the immaculate mansions of multimillionaires.

The Church of St Brelade

Churches of St Brelade

Away from the crowds at the far west of the bay, the parish **Church of St Brelade** overlooks the tiny harbour. The large churchyard was formerly the burial place of more than 300 Germans, some of whom had been prisoners here in World War I, others who had served during the more recent German Occupation. The bodies were exhumed in the early 1960s and given a final resting place at a military cemetery in St Malo across the water. The pink granite church dates back to the 11th and 12th centuries, and still retains Norman features. As you go in switch on the lights at the left of the entrance to reveal the enchanting interior with its warm granite walls. Embedded within them are stones from the beach and limpet shells.

Just next door to the church is the lovely **Fishermen's Chapel,** also built of local granite and dating back to Nor-

10

One of numerous varieties of lavender

man times. Following the Reformation it fell into disuse for some 300 years, and was variously used as an armoury, store room and carpenter's shop. Restoration in the early 20th century revealed a series of medieval frescoes depicting scenes from the Old and New Testaments. Only fragments remain but information boards fill in the gaps so you can make out the scenes. The most complete and the oldest fresco is the *Annunciation* on the east wall, which includes the members of the donor's family kneeling on either side of the Virgin and Archangel.

Jersey Lavender Farm

11 ▶ Follow your nose inland from St Brelade's Bay for the **Jersey Lavender Farm** (Rue du Pon Marquet, St Brelade's; end May–end Sep Tue–Sun 10am–5pm; charge), whose 9 acres (3.6 hectares) of sweet-scented lavender resemble a little patch of Provence. The garden contains around 80 different varieties of lavenders, plus more than 100 different varieties of culinary, medicinal, aromatic and dyers' herbs. The lavender is cut by hand, distilled on site and the essential oils matured and blended with other ingredients to produce eau de toilettes and colognes, soap and lotions and lavender bags. A video presentation shows all the stages of production and in summer talks on the distillation process are given at 11.30am and 3pm. The best time to visit is between early June and late July/early

August when the lavender is in flower – at other times of year the admission charge is substantially reduced. Lavender products are on sale in the shop – for a list of all the therapeutic usages of lavender oil go to the website on www.jerseylavender.co.uk – and for lavender-flavoured savoury dishes, scones and short bread, try Sprigs Café next to the shop.

Beauport

The steep road westwards from St Brelade's Bay takes you to **Beauport**, the islanders' favourite beach. Hidden away from the main road, entailing a longish trek down a steep hill, this beautiful sheltered bay is totally unspoilt. The waters here are crystal clear, the soft sands washed by the tides and unspoilt by beach facilities. There is not even a drinks kiosk, let alone parasols – so remember to take your own provisions, along with suncream.

Beauport Beach

The Corbière Lighthouse

THE WEST COAST

This is Jersey's wildest coast, with waves crashing around Corbière Lighthouse and Atlantic surf pounding the huge beach of St Ouen's. This 4-mile (6.5-km) arc of sand stretches almost the entire length of the west coast. Behind the beach a large expanse of unspoilt sand dunes is home to a wealth of flora and fauna.

La Corbière

12 Sitting atop the jagged rocks **Corbière Lighthouse** is one of Jersey's most familiar landmarks and a favourite spot from which to watch sunsets and rough seas. The name Corbière derives from *corbeau* (crow), traditionally seen as a bird of ill omen, and this wild and desolate tip of the island is inextricably linked with tales of shipwrecks and smuggling. The first recorded ship to flounder on the rocks here was a

Spanish vessel in 1495 carrying a cargo of wine. The seigneur of St Ouen was entitled by Jersey law to shipwrecked vessels and their cargo, and it is said that smugglers worked alongside the seigneur, luring ships on to the treacherous rocks with lanterns, which looked like the lights of vessels on the open sea. Among other casualties at Corbière was the Royal Mail Steam Packet, which was shipwrecked on the rocks in 1859. A lighthouse was finally erected here in 1874 – the first one in the British Isles to be made of reinforced concrete rather than stone. Weather permitting, the light beam can be seen up to a distance of 18 miles (29km). The lighthouse is closed to the public apart from those on organised guided walks (see www.jersey.com/walking).

At mid to low tide you can cross the causeway to the lighthouse, but check the tides before doing so and heed the siren which sounds when the waters start galloping up over the rocks. The monument of two clasped hands on the headland commemorates the rescue in 1995 of the French catamaran, *Saint Malo*, which ran aground when travelling from Jersey to Sark. All 307

Rooms with a view

Set on the cliff top overlooking Corbière Lighthouse, the massive concrete observation tower was built during the German Occupation in World War II. Restored in Modernist Bauhaus style, the six-floor tower, with terrific 360 degree views from the panoramic windows of the penthouse, is now rented out by Jersey Heritage as stylish self-catering accommodation.

Low tide reveals seaweed at St Ouen's Bay

passengers were saved. A carved stone on the causeway recalls a story with a less happy outcome: an assistant lighthouse keeper who drowned while trying to save a tourist who was caught by the incoming tide.

St Ouen's Bay

This huge sandy beach is Jersey's surfing hotspot. While La Pulente at the southern end is protected from the Atlantic swell, the big rollers further north provide championship conditions. Surf schools dotted along the bay hire out equipment for windsurfing, bodyboarding and skim-boarding as well as surfing. Inexperienced surfers should always keep between the red and yellow flags, where Australian lifeguards patrol. A couple of cafés provide seaview terraces where you can simply sit and watch the pros at play. (Big Vern's has great views and is the best bet for hearty breakfasts, lunches or sunset suppers.)

13 ▶ On a rocky islet at the southern end of the bay **La Rocco Tower** was one of nine round towers that were constructed along the bay during the Napoleonic Wars. The tower took a battering during the Occupation in World War II when the Germans used it as target practice, but it has since undergone restoration. The concrete wall backing the entire bay was built by slave labourers of the Todt Organisation against tanks coming ashore from Allied landing craft. Today the west-facing wall is a useful barrier during spring tides, and provides a warm, wind-free screen for sunbathers. The spacious sands here are favourite spots among islanders for post-surf BBQs, ideally as the sun is setting.

At the southern end of the bay **Les Blanches Banques** sand dunes, with abundant marram grass, are a haven for naturalists. Rare invertebrates such as the large Jersey green lizard, the blue winged grasshopper and bloody-nosed beetle can be found here. More than 400 plant species have been recorded, no fewer than 16 of them featuring in the British red data book of endangered species.

In 1914 Jersey was called on to build a prisoner-of-war camp to accommodate 1,000 German prisoners. This was built on the lower dune plain, and by 1917 had expanded to

Stocking up on Seaweed

If you happen to be on the beach in autumn or winter you may see tractors loading up with vraic (pronounced 'rack') from the beach. This is the seaweed which for centuries has been used to fertilise farms bordering the coast. There are two types of vraic: the weed washed up on the beach after stormy weather, and the type cut from the rocks, which was used as fuel by fishermen who could not afford coal or wool. Vraic collection days were party-like with whole families gathering on the beaches, men wading out to the rocks on foot or going by boat, while women and children collected ormers, crabs and limpets in profusion. Spirits were kept high with vraic buns and cider, and at the end of the day the seaweed was brought up from the bay by horse and cart, and families returned home to feast on shellfish. Cutting of vraic from the rocks was only allowed at certain times of year, and was closely supervised by parish officials. Today there are no restrictions on the public removing seaweed and it is permitted to take a vehicle on to the beach for this purpose.

Kempt Tower Visitor Centre

take in 1,500 prisoners. The camp was closed in 1919.

Further north **Le Noir Pré** meadows, accessed from the Chemin de L'Ouzière, are one of the last strongholds of the loose-flowered or Jersey orchid (*Orchis laxiflora*). Guernsey is the only other place in the British Isles where the orchid can be found. In May to mid-June the meadows are a riot of colour from these and other flowering orchids. The reed beds and marshy surrounds of the nearby St Ouen's Pond (La Mare au Seigneur) draw scores of migratory birds, including sedge warblers and bearded reedlings. Marsh harriers can often be seen drifting over the reed beds.

 You can find further information on the area at the **Kempt Tower Visitor Centre** (May–Sept daily 2–5pm; charge), a stocky, circular tower overlooking the bay, with great views from the top. Run by the Department of the Environment, this centre focuses on the ecology of the bay, with several hands-on displays. New additions are a military section and an exhibition on the story of surfing.

Channel Islands Military Museum

The Grande Route des Mielles (otherwise known as Five Mile Road, even though it's less than four) leads north to a clutch of visitor attractions. Above the beach a World War II German bunker is home to the **Channel Islands Military Museum** (Easter–Oct daily 10am–5pm; charge), devoted to German Occupation memorabilia. Exhibits include arms and ammunition, Luftwaffe brass band instruments, tins of dried eggs from Red Cross food parcels and a stark notice of the sentence of death of a Jersey resident for releasing a pigeon with a message for England.

Across the main road charabancs disgorge visitors at **Jersey Pearl**, where you can learn all about pearls, watch the craftsmen and tour the plush showroom.

L'Etacq

The B35 then heads inland, passing en route **Treasures of the Earth** (Mar–Oct daily 10am–5pm; charge), a crystal cave exhibition and a large shop packed with fossils, minerals and bronze sculpture.

The road drops down to Le Grand Etaquerel, a vast expanse of reefs whose main attraction is the **Faulkner Fisheries** which sell fresh Jersey seafood from an ex-German bunker on a rocky promontory. The bunker overlooks **Le Pulec Bay**, known familiarly as Stinky Bay for reasons that will soon become apparent. The odorous seaweed is still used to fertilise some of the Jersey Royal potatoes grown on the steeply sloping hillsides *(côtils)* on the landward side.

The windswept clifftops between L'Etacq and Grosnez provide some spectacular views along the coastline. The main road diverts inland

Fresh seafood at Faulkner Fisheries

after L'Etacq but you can pick up a footpath to the top of the cliffs. Wartime relics include restored gun emplacements and bunkers from the **Moltke Battery,** which once sprawled across the headland here. (Open some Sundays; for information visit www.ciosjersey.org.uk). Perched right above the sea **16** on rapidly eroding cliffs is **Le Pinacle**, a 200-ft (60-m) high menhir-like stack, used as an ancient ceremonial site from the Neolithic to Roman eras. Brooding on the clifftops to the north is the **MP3** direction and range-finding tower, another potent symbol of the German Occupation. Inland the extensive windswept heath, known as **Les Landes**, is home to Jersey's racecourse, a rifle range and an airfield for model aircraft.

Grosnez Castle

17 On the northwest tip of the island, the ruins of **Grosnez Castle** stand evocatively on the heather- and gorse-clad clifftops. This was a 14th-century fortification believed to have been destroyed by the French in the same century. On a clear day you can spot all the other Channel Islands from the castle ruins. Going from left to right these are Guernsey, Jethou, Herm and Sark, with Alderney in the far distance and the coast of Normandy to the east. At low tide you can see an extensive reef, known as the Paternoster, offshore to the east. Local legend relates that in the 16th century a boatload of women and children, who were en route to colonise Sark, were shipwrecked on the treacherous rocks here. Superstitious sailors would recite the Lord's Prayer when rounding the reef, hence the name.

Le Pinacle

Colourful cottages at Rozel

THE NORTH COAST

The wild and rugged north coast, where heather and gorse-clad cliffs tower above tiny sheltered harbours, couldn't be more of a contrast to the flat beaches and calm seas of the south. The peaceful north coast footpath *(see page 90)*, stretching all the way from Grosnez in the west to Rozel in the east, is the most exhilarating walk on the island, affording spectacular sea views. The paths, flanked by wild flowers, dip down to little bays, where you can take a break at harbour-side cafés or cool off in clear waters.

Plémont

The most westerly beach is **Plémont** or, more correctly, La Grève au Lançon (Sand Eel Beach). At high tide the beach is non-existent, but twice a day the waters recede to reveal an unspoilt expanse of golden sands. This is by far the best

18

Puffins at Plémont

The burrows in the cliffs near the abandoned holiday village at Plémont have been the nesting site of a small colony of puffins for more than a century. From around 1,000 pairs in the 1950s the number has now dwindled to just a dozen. Climate change and food shortages, particularly the declining number of sand eels, are thought to be the causes. You will only be able to spot the puffins if you come in spring when they are nesting.

beach on the north coast, and the longish flight of steps down and the lack of facilities keep away the crowds. The seas can get rough here, and it's popular with surfers, but normally in summer it's safe enough for bathing, and lifeguards patrol the beach for most of the day. Behind the beach the sea has eroded the cliffs, there are caves to explore and rock pools for paddling. The **Plémont Beach Café** at the top of the steps is an excellent spot for a bite, using prime Jersey produce. Parking just above the bay, where cars are lined up on the steep and narrow road, is best avoided in season. It's easier to leave your car near the bus stop at the top and take the scenic cliff path down to the beach, enjoying the views as you go.

On the headland above the beach sits a crumbling post-war holiday camp, which later became Pontins and then fell into disuse. The building was bought recently and 73 apartments are in the pipeline. The project has given rise to major controversy, with locals campaigning for the building to be demolished and the restoration of the headland to a natural state.

Grève de Lecq

Going eastwards Grève de Lecq (well signed off the B55) is the most popular of the north coast bays, with a large car park to accommodate island tour buses, a sandy beach, fishing pier and choice of eateries. Up from the bay the **Grève de Lecq Barracks** (May–Sept Wed–Sat 10am–5pm, Sun 1–5pm) were built in 1810–15 in preparation for an expected Napoleonic invasion. British troops were garrisoned here until the 1920s. The only surviving barracks on the island, they have been restored by Jersey's National Trust, and are used as the North Coast Visitor Centre and a military museum with dormitories, officers' quarters and store rooms. Parts of the barracks are now being turned into self-catering accommodation for tourists.

In a valley up the road the **Moulin de Lecq** is the place for a pint *(see page 111)*, either in the garden or in the olde

Moulin de Lecq

worlde bar where the huge cog of this former water mill provides an unusual backdrop. The great water wheel outside still functions, though it is no longer used to grind flour. During the German Occupation the water wheel was used to power energy for searchlights to defend the bay.

The promontory east of the bay, known as **Le Câtel de Lecq**, was an Iron Age earthwork fortification, where Gallic and Roman coins were discovered. Beyond, a remote beach, **Le Val Rouget**, can be accessed via a cliff path and a long dark tunnel, which you can only pass through at very low tide. The route goes via **Venus' Pool**, where you can jump from a high rock into the deep, dark waters. Youngsters love the adventure but check with locals about the tides and the route before setting off.

La Mare vines

La Mare Wine Estate

From Grève de Lecq the B40 takes you to the village of St Mary; from here follow signs for the Devil's Hole to reach **La Mare Wine Estate** ◄ 20 (Apr–Oct daily 10am–5pm; charge; www.lamarevineyards. com; guided tours every 45 mins from 10.45am–3.30pm). From a small family-run tourist attraction this has expanded into a professionally managed 25-acre (10-hectare) estate, producing a range of wines, ciders and spirits – along with a large range of Jersey culinary specialities.

The estate is centred around an old granite farmhouse and tours cover the vineyards and orchards, distillery, chocolate kitchen and a tasting session. Forty thousand bottles are produced annually, including sparkling wines, made according to the *méthode Champenoise*, and a range of still whites and reds. Most of the cider made here is double distilled

Traditional Jersey delicacy

in a Cognac brandy pot and aged in oak casks to become Jersey apple brandy. The vineyard shop stocks black butter *(see page 105)*, preserves and luxury chocolates as well as wines; a restaurant, with vineyard-view terrace, is open for coffee, cream teas and lunches; alternatively you can order a French-style picnic on arrival, to eat in the vineyards.

Devil's Hole

From the Priory Inn car park just north of La Mare a footpath leads down to the cliffs and Le Creux de Vis (Screw Hole) or, as it's more familiarly known, **Devil's Hole.** From a narrow causeway you can watch the waves crash into a yawning chasm in the cliff as the tides come up. This blowhole was created by the sea eroding the roof of what was once a cave. The dramatic name of Devil's Hole was acquired in the 19th century and is believed to have originated from the shipwreck of a French boat in 1851. The figurehead of the vessel was discovered in the hole here, and a local sculptor transformed it into a wooden devil with horns. A replica of the original towers over the pond beside the path that winds down to the Devil's Hole.

Bonne Nuit

Sheltering below the heather-clad cliffs, the next bay is picturesque **Bonne Nuit** (Good Night). The name was recorded back in the 12th century, refuting the long-held belief that it derived from King Charles II's parting words *Bonne nuit, belle Jersey*, when he left from the port here after his exile on the island. The name probably referred to the shelter that the little harbour offered to sailors overnight.

The unspoilt bay comprises little more than a stone jetty sheltering the harbour, a sand, shingle and rock beach taken up by little fishing boats that go out daily for lobsters and crabs, and the popular **Bonne Nuit Beach Café** with lovely views of the bay. A familiar sight at low or mid tide is the gaggle of ducks waddling across the beach, hopeful of a crumb from the cream teas served up by the café.

On the rugged headland east of the bay the British-built **La Crête Fort** (1830) used to be a weekend retreat for the island's lieutenant-governor. Now anyone can holiday here through Jersey Heritage. There are a couple of simply-furnished bedrooms, wonderful views over open seas to Guernsey, Sark and the coast of France, and a secluded walled garden where you can sit and contemplate the sunset.

Boats at Bonne Nuit

J 258

Bouley Bay

Two other historic forts, built in the line of defence against the French, have been converted for holiday lets at **Bouley Bay** to the southeast. Fort Leicester (named after Queen Elizabeth I's earl of Leicester) sleeps up to eight. The more basic L'Etacquerel Fort has 'stone hut' accommodation for 30 – and space for 60 by day. Accessed via a steep coastal path, and a high wooden bridge over the moat, this is a peaceful atmospheric spot for a back-to-basics gathering. There are no utilities (composting toilets only) and you bring your own sleeping bag.

Bouley Bay consists of no more than a steeply shelving pebble and rock beach (voted one of the cleanest in the UK), the Water's Edge Hotel, **Black Dog Pub** and a diving school. With its deep, clear and pond-like waters, this is the main place on Jersey for scuba diving. It's also a good spot for kayaking, swimming, snorkelling – or just sitting at **Mad Mary's Café** right on the beach and enjoying the views. Bouley Bay is the venue for the British Hill Climb Championships, and three times a year the peace of the bay is shattered as saloon cars, racing cars, sports cars and motor bikes race up the steep hill.

Fearsome hound

Jersey abounds with myth and superstition. On the north coast tales used to spread of the Black Dog of Bouley Bay, a terrifying beast with huge teeth and eyes the size of saucers that roamed the coastline. The tales were probably invented by smugglers hoping to scare away parishioners from the coast while they landed their cargoes of brandy and tobacco.

Rozel

24 Nestling below wooded slopes, **Rozel** is a romantic little creek, with a handful of fishermen's cottages, a small port and shingle beach. There has always been a fishing harbour here, and in the 1820s there were around 30 oyster-fishing boats based here. Today fishermen go out for lobster and crab (the Hungry Man kiosk by the pier serves a great crab sandwich and a 50p mug of tea). Behind the bay barracks were built in 1810 but the anticipated attack on Rozel never took place – despite it being the closest point on the island to France. The barracks were converted into a hotel but this has closed down and is to be converted into luxury apartments.

Behind the bay the **Vallée de Rozel** is lush and verdant, planted with subtropical trees and shrubs. Tucked away in the valley is the elegant **Château La Chaire Hotel** *(see page 138)* with over 8 acres (3 hectares) of beautiful gardens and grounds, created by Samuel Curtis, a 19th-century botanist and former director of Kew Gardens. Curtis first saw the site in 1841 and, having searched all over the British Isles, instantly knew that this steep-sided valley, with a stream running onto the shingle beach of Rozel Bay, was the ideal spot for his subtropical plant paradise. He built a small house here under the cliffs and created a series of paths and terraces. The house was pulled down at the end of the century, and a grander one took its place (now the hotel). During the Occupation the Germans dug up some of the prized trees, and today few of Curtis' original species survive.

Speckled wood butterfly in Vallée de Rozel

Flamingoes at the Durrell Wildlife Conservation Trust

DURRELL

'The world is as delicate and as complicated as a spider's web. If you touch one thread you send shudders running through all the other threads. We are not just touching the webs, we are tearing great holes in it...' Gerald Durrell (author and naturalist).

Gerald Durrell's first intelligible word is said to have been 'zoo'. From the age of six he had wanted to create a safe place for his collection of animals. In 1959, 34 years later, he realised his childhood dream by creating Jersey Zoo. It was set up not as a zoo in the conventional sense but as a sanctuary and breeding centre for some of the world's most endangered animal species. Durrell's objectives were to provide a safe haven for these rare species, build up colonies, then send them to organisations worldwide, who would return them to the wild and reintroduce them to areas where they had become extinct.

Durrell chose the dodo as symbol of the zoo, demonstrating his commitment to saving rare species from the fate of the flightless bird from Mauritius. The original name of Jersey Zoo was changed to the **Durrell Wildlife Conservation Trust** (daily 9.30am–6pm, until 5pm off-season; charge; www.durrellwildlife.org; bus routes Nos 3a, 3b and 23; bike routes 3a, 1 or 1b), otherwise known simply as 'Durrell'. Since 1977 conservationists from around the world have been trained in the theory and practice of endangered species recovery, and the trust has earned a worldwide reputation for pioneering conservation techniques. Durrell died in 1995. His widow, zoologist Dr Lee Durrell, continues his dedicated work at the trust.

Gerald Durrell

Gerald Durrell was born in India and from an early age he collected 'everything from minnows to woodlice'. After the death of his father, when Gerald was only 3 years old, his mother brought him and his sister to England to be educated. Durrell detested school, left at the age of 9, and was educated by private tutors who concentrated on what he loved: natural history. Four idyllic years from the age of 10 were spent in Corfu, surrounded by a menagerie of animals. This led to his best-known novel, *My Family and Other Animals* (1956), which has sold five million copies. His early working years were spent in a pet shop in London, on a farm near Bournemouth and for a year as student keeper at Whipsnade Zoo. At 21 he inherited £3,000, which funded his first animal collection expedition – to the British Cameroons – and he spent the next decade collecting animals and selling them to British zoos. Durrell wrote 33 books, hosted TV series and radio programmes, and won nine international awards for leadership in conservation.

Conservation mainly focuses on the island areas of the Galápagos, the Caribbean islands, Madagascar and Indian Ocean islands and India – but not forgetting Jersey's own dwindling amphibians such as the agile frog and the common toad (or *crapaud*), the island's beloved mascot. Among the species that have been pulled back from the brink are the pink pigeons and kestrels from Mauritius, the St Lucia whiptail, the thick-billed parrots from Arizona, and the pygmy hog, the world's oldest and rarest pig, which has been successfully reintroduced to the wildlife sanctuary in Assam, northeast India. In the late 1980s a

One of Durrell's silver-back lowland gorillas

couple of St Lucia parrots flew back to the Caribbean with British Airways, accompanied by the prime minister of St Lucia who had come to Jersey specifically to escort them home. Recent projects include the Jamaican boa or yellowsnake, the Madagascan teal and flat-tailed tortoise, the Floreana mocking bird from the Galápagos and the Montserrat mountain chicken, which is in fact a large frog, tasting of chicken. The latter is endangered by a deadly fungal disease discovered on the Carribean island.

If you're expecting unhappy animals cramped in cages you're in for a pleasant surprise. The setting is a 32-acre (13 hectare) oasis of woodland, landscaped lawns and water gar-

A marmoset

dens, surrounding an 18th-century granite manor house. Wherever possible the trust has tried to cultivate the native habitat for family groups of the endangered species. Certainly by average zoo standards, the animals do look remarkably content. The golden-headed lion tamarins roam in the woods, the gorillas play in a spacious compound, flamingoes wade in the lake, reptiles have their own tropical habitat-simulated quarters, aye-ayes have a special nocturnal unit, orang-utans swing from ropes or stick twigs in logs to prise out the honey.

Among the favourite residents are the silver-back lowland gorillas descended from Jambo, the 'gentle giant' who hit the headlines in 1986 when he protected a 5-year-old boy who fell into the compound. Jambo was the first male gorilla to be reared in captivity. He died in 1992 and his successor is the 25-year-old, 520-lb (235-kg), Ya Kwanza.

THE EAST COAST

Star attractions of the east coast are Mont Orgueil Castle, a majestic fortress that played a pivotal role in the island's history, and the picturesque port of Gorey, which shelters beneath its walls. From here the Royal Bay of Grouville, sheltered from westerly winds, stretches southwards for nearly 2 miles (3km). Queen Victoria was so impressed by the spacious, sandy bay that she added the royal prefix after her visit in 1859.

St Catherine's Breakwater

The most significant feature of **St Catherine's Bay** is the massive **breakwater** which encloses it on the northern side. ◄ 26 In response to coastal installations, which the French had created at Cherbourg, the British decided to build a naval base with a large deepwater harbour at St Catherine's. Warnings that the waters were too shallow for warships went unheeded and in 1847 breakwaters were built both here and at Archirondel Tower to the south. By the time the St Catherine's breakwater was complete, eight years on, the British realised their blunder and the project was abandoned. Today the breakwater provides a bracing half-mile (0.8-km) walk, a shelter for dinghies and a useful pier for anglers. From the lighthouse at the end there are fine views of the coast to the south, the small pebble and rock bay of Fliquet to the north, which you can reach on foot, and the rocky islets known as

Anne Port, in the south of St Catherine's Bay

Les Écréhous *(see panel below)*. On a clear day you can see as far as the Normandy coast.

Just south of the breakwater a **German bunker** houses tanks of around 6,500 turbot, ranging from tiddlers to mature 2½-lb (1-kg) fish. The larger ones are sold to restaurateurs, fishmongers and the public. There are guided tours on request (minimum five people; charge, tel: 01534 868836).

From St Catherine's Bay you can walk all the way to Gorey – or drive on the coastal B29. A distinctive landmark is the red and white **Archirondel Tower** on the eponymous beach, built in 1792 as a garrison for artillery soldiers. The tower has recently been restored and is now available for 'stone hut' holiday accommodation. Inland, a walk through **St Catherine's Wood** provides a delightful shady diversion from the coast.

Geoffrey's Leap

The rocky promontory between Anne Port Bay and Gorey Harbour is known as Le Saut Geoffroi or **Geoffrey's Leap**,

Kings of Les Écréhous

The reef of rocks lying mid-way between Jersey and Normandy, known as Les Écréhous, has been part of Jersey's bailiwick since 1953. The reef expands by about 80 percent at low tide and it's a lovely spot to visit on a boat trip in season. A couple of 'kings' have inhabited the reef: in 1848 Phillipe Pinel lived with his wife on Blanche Île for 46 years and was proclaimed 'king' by local fishermen who lived in the huts here. In the 1960s Alphonse Le Gastelois, an eccentric fisherman and farmhand who was suspected of being the mystery child attacker known as 'the beast of Jersey', moved to Les Écréhous and lived alone here for 14 years, claiming that the island belonged to him. (By the time he returned to Jersey, the real beast, one Edward Paisnel, had been tracked down, convicted of 13 counts of assault, rape and sodomy and sentenced to 30 years' imprisonment.)

La Pouquelaye de Faldouet

after a popular Jersey legend. A renowned womaniser, Geoffrey was convicted of sexual harrassment and sentenced to be thrown off the cliffs here on to the rocks below. Miraculously he missed the rocks and surfaced at Anne Port to the north. The reaction among islanders was divided: some wanted him thrown off the cliffs again, others, including some female admirers, saw his survival as proof of innocence. Seeing another opportunity to impress local women, Geoffrey took it upon himself to repeat the leap – but this time he hurled himself to destruction.

Off a country lane inland from Geoffrey's Leap and approached along a leafy path is **La Pouquelaye de Faldouet**, ◀ **28** an impressive and somewhat elusive 50-ft (15-m) long neolithic passage grave. Dolmens like these played an important role in the rich folklore of the island, and this one, tucked away off a rural lane, retains an air of mysterious antiquity. Look on any Jersey 10p coin and you will see a picture of it.

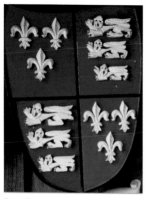

Recalling the days of old

Mont Orgueil Castle

Even if you have never visited **Mont Orgueil Castle** ◄ 29
(Apr–Oct daily 10am–dusk,
Nov–Mar Fri–Mon; charge),
it is likely to look familiar.
Symbolic of Jersey, the pho-
togenic fortress is reproduced
on countless postcards, holiday brochures and guides.
Commanding a spectacular
promontory above the har-
bour, built into the granite
rocks, it makes a wonderful
backdrop to Gorey Harbour,
both by day and by night
when the battlements are floodlit.

The earliest fortifications date back to the very early 13th
century when King John had lost control of Normandy and
the island needed protection against the threat of French invasion. Built in a concentric series of defences, the castle
proved to be an impregnable fortress. As warfare changed
the fortification was expanded and strengthened. Fifteen
French attacks were made between 1204 and 1600, most of
them unsuccessful. One notable exception was the French
invasion of 1468 which resulted in a seven-year occupation.

Mont Orgueil was essentially a bow-and-arrow castle and
by the late 16th century it was no longer able to sustain modern warfare. Elizabeth Castle, equipped with cannons, was
built on Jersey's south coast. Mont Orgueil would have been
razed to the ground were it not for the intervention of Sir
Walter Raleigh, then governor of the island, who decided
that the stately fort should stay. It became a prison in the
17th century, then in 1789 a refuge for aristocrats fleeing the

reign of terror and the guillotine in France. In 1907 the castle was finally given by the Crown to the States of Jersey and in 1996 Queen Elizabeth II handed it over to the islanders.

A network of ancient, dark staircases and cobbled passageways lead up to lofty ramparts. At the top Somerset Tower, adapted under the German Occupation as an observation post, commands magnificent 360 degree views of the island and across to France. Within the castle there is plenty to explore in the way of medieval keeps, cellars, towers, chapels and gun platforms. History is kept alive with audio-visual presentations, large artworks (such as the gruesome carving showing the fate that might await those defending the castle from attack), twice-weekly hawking demonstrations and occasional tales and displays of Tudor life. The castle also makes a perfect backdrop for occasional medieval drama and re-enactments.

Mont Orgueil Castle

Gorey Harbour

Gorey

Below the castle walls **Gorey Harbour** is a picture post-card ensemble of quaint houses, pubs and seafood cafés, clustering around a harbour of fishing boats, yachts and pleasure craft. In the early 19th century the port grew prosperous on the oyster trade, becoming known as 'the pearl of the east'. The British muscled in on the lucrative industry and by the 1830s there were around 260 oyster vessels and 1,400 fishermen – along with 600–700 women and children who gave a helping hand. Fishing cottages were built at Gorey and a pier to protect the oyster fleet. But the fishermen became overambitious and by the 1860s the oyster beds were almost exhausted. The village returned to its shellfish-producing traditions by introducing oyster and mussel farms in the last century. More than 4 million oysters are now produced annually – and not surprisingly, they feature on virtually every Gorey menu.

You can discover more about the history of the oyster trade at **Discovery Pier** (May–Sept daily 10am–4pm; charge) at the end of Gorey Pier. This informative little hands-on museum, run by the Department of the Environment, focuses on marine life. In season catamarans, run by Manches-Îles Express, depart from the pier for day trips to the Norman port of Carteret.

Jersey Pottery

From the small tourist attraction which opened in 1946 **Jersey Pottery** (Gorey Village; daily but no production on Mon; free; www.jerseypottery.com) has grown into a a highly organised commercial enterprise. It exports to 20 countries, designs crockery for Harrods restaurants and has created a bespoke range for the world's first 7-star hotel in Abu Dhabi. But pottery is only part of the business. The ever-expanding empire runs half a dozen restaurants and cafés on the island plus a gastropub. Outside catering is also big business.

◀ ❸⓿

Three generations of the same family have run the pottery since 1954. Visitors can watch the processes of pottery production, from the raw clay (which comes from Devon and Cornwall) to decorating and glazing, and visit the showroom. The pottery is located in Gorey Village, signed from the main A3 going south to St Helier.

The Royal Bay of Grouville

The huge expanse of sands stretching south from Gorey Harbour attracts water sports aficionados, joggers, sunbathers and swimmers. Bathing is safe but with the huge tidal movement you should be prepared for quite a walk out to sea. In July and August the Gorey Watersports Centre organises kayaking, water-skiing, wakeboarding, speedboat rides and self-drive motor dinghies – wetsuits, life-jackets and tuition are all provided.

Plates from Jersey Pottery

During World War II the Germans used a million tons of Grouville sand to con-

Sea shells at La Rocque Point

struct the concrete fortifications around the coast. To facilitate its transport, a railway line (no longer extant) was built from Gorey to St Helier. The spacious Grouville Common that borders the beach saw duels fought in the 18th century, and horse racing in Victorian times. If you're strolling on the common watch out for stray golf balls. This is home to the exclusive Royal Jersey Golf Club, where Grouville-born Harry Vardon (six times British Open Championship winner) trained in the early years. Vardon was the first professional golfer to play in knickerbockers and is famous for the overlapping grip which bears his name and which is used by the vast majority of golfers. The club has been here since 1878 (when it opened as the Grouville Golf Club) and remained unchanged until the German Occupation when the links were transformed into a minefield. Today the club is the most exclusive on the island. Visitors are welcome provided they are members of a recognised golf club.

Seymour Tower

The predominantly rocky shoreline to the south of Grouville Bay is guarded by a series of towers, built in the 18th century but never actually used to defend the island. Some of the towers have been turned into private residences. At the southeastern tip **La Rocque Harbour** was the arrival point of Baron de Rullecourt and his troops, who made a surprise night-time landing in 1781, only to be defeated in the Battle of Jersey *(see page 21)*. At low tide you can walk out to Seymour Tower, isolated on a rocky islet 2 miles (3km) at the southern end of Grouville Bay. The walk takes you over an eerie wilderness of gullies, sandbars, reefs and rocks and the low-lying coast provides a rich breeding ground for thousands of wintering waders, gulls and wildfowl. Watch out for the tides – the sea comes galloping in at a frighteningly fast rate.

Those with a sense of adventure might like to stay overnight in **Seymour Tower**, which can accommodate up to six guests, sleeping in bunk beds. There are no luxuries like running water but drinking water is provided, as are logs for the wood burning stove. You carry your own food, clothes and sleeping bags out to the tower. The only hitch, at least for independently minded visitors, is that you must be accompanied by a Seymour Tower Guide who guides you to and from the tower and stays the night. (For further information, go to www.jerseyheritage.org.)

The Seymour Tower at low tide

WHAT TO DO

SPORTS

Big surfing beaches, rock-bound coves, clear diving waters and gently shelving sands make for a wide range of aquatic activities. Traditional sports, such as sailing, surfing and water-skiing, have been joined in recent years by new adrenalin-fuelled activities such as blokarting, skydiving, abseiling, coasteering and kiteboarding. Add to these boat trips, fishing, five golf courses, stylish new spas and gyms, and there's enough action for any sports and fitness enthusiast. There are around 20 sports and activity operators on the island – check the Jersey Tourism website: www.jersey.com.

Water Sports

Surfing. With towering Atlantic rollers and a huge beach, St Ouen's bay on the west coast, is *the* place to surf. The Jersey Surfboard Club, one of the oldest in Europe, celebrated its 50th anniversary in 2009 with the European Surfing Championships. Surf schools can arrange equipment hire and give you advice on how to ride the rollers. Unless you're a real pro, keep to the areas between the yellow and red flags, which are surveyed by lifeguards. Bodyboarding and windsurfing equipment are also available, though beginner windsurfers are better off at St Brelade's, St Aubin's or Grouville where the waters are calmer. High-octane thrill-seekers can try kitesurfing, where you use a surfboard and large kite to propel yourself at high speed across the ocean. Lessons are available for people over 16 (www.kiteschooljersey.com). To get safely up and running on a kitesurf takes around three two-hour sessions over the course of a few days. The location depends on which way the wind is blowing.

Wakeboarding and Water-skiing. The latest craze is wakeboarding, which is likened to snow-boarding on water, with a speedboat pulling you through the waves. You can try it out at St Brelade's Bay, St Aubin's Bay and the Royal Bay of Grouville. The best spots for water-skiing are St Aubin's Bay and Grouville, where the waters are not too choppy.

Sailing. Marinas and harbours have excellent facilities for sailors but beginners should beware of sunken reefs, big tides and strong currents. Experienced sailors can charter boats or join local regattas. **Jersey Sailing** (tel: 01534 747738, www.jerseysailing.com) is the main centre on the island, offering power and sailboat charter, tuition at all levels and challenging racing weekends for the experienced. Flexible day or evening sailing trips, focusing on marine life and the heritage of Icho and Seymour towers and Les Ecréhous, are organised by **Sealife Sailing** (tel: 01534 32060, www.

Braving the surf in St Ouen's Bay

sealifesailing.co.uk), who
sail from Gorey Harbour.
The catamaran can be char-
tered for up to five passengers, and individuals or
couples can often share trips
with others; if not, it works
out very expensive. For day
trips to other channel Islands, or overnight trips to
French ports on a Sigma 33
cruiser-racer contact **Raleigh
Sailing** (tel: 01534 607910,
www.raleighsailing.com).

The Polar Bears

The seawater swimming
enthusiasts known as 'The
Polar Bears' meet at Havre
des Pas Bathing Pool for
daily swims throughout
summer, and weekly ones
in winter. These Jersey residents welcome visitors to
join them. Depending on
the sea temperature it
might be a quick dip or a
mile-long swim around the
bay (tel: 01534 870788).

Sea kayaking/Coasteering. Jersey's clear waters, remote
coves and rich marine life make for excellent kayaking and
coasteering (scrambling around the rocks, cliff jumping
and swimming through caves). Kayaks can be hired at the
main beaches. A half-day expedition of seakayaking and
coasteering can be organised through **Pure Adventure**
(www.purejersey.com).

Diving. Bouley Bay, with its clear, calm waters, is the most
popular part of the island for scuba diving. The **Bouley Bay
Diving School** (www.scuabdivingjersey. com), which is over
50 years old, welcomes beginners and experts alike. Divers
with experience can dive down to wrecks of ships sunk in
World War II and other vessels that have been deliberately
scuttled to provide shelter for marine life.

Swimming. If you don't mind coolish waters Jersey can be
idyllic for swimming. Sea temperatures average around 17°C
(63°F) in summer, which deters most beachgoers and, once
past the paddlers, you can have huge expanses of clear seawater all to yourself. Beware, however, of heavy swells and
swimming on incoming tides. Lifeguards patrol St Ouen's

Blokarting

It's not only adrenalin junkies who practise this fast and furious sport. It doesn't take long to grasp the basics and you don't have to go at 55mph (88kmph), the maximum speed. The blokart, a three-wheeled kart with a large sail, propels you along the beach. You steer the cart with one hand, and control the speed with the other.

beach, St Brelade's Bay, Plémont and some of the other main beaches from mid-May to the end of September. The patrolled areas are indicated by red and yellow flags. Red flags indicate that sea conditions are dangerous.

Fishing. There is still plenty of marine life around the Jersey shores. From rocks, breakwaters and harbours anglers can fish for black bream, mullet, bass, wrasse and conger. For day or evening boat fishing trips from St Helier contact David Nuth, tel: 01534 858046 or 07797 728316 (www.tarkaseatrips.com). Low tide is the best time for fishing for crabs, prawns and devil fish in the rock pools. Freshwater anglers can try their luck fly-fishing for trout as well as coarse fishing (www.jersey.com/fishing).

Land Sports

Golf. Jersey has no fewer than six golf courses and an impressive pedigree. Harry Vardon, six-times winner of the British Open, was born here, and Ian Woosnam is an island resident. Proof of handicap is required at the 18-hole championship courses: **La Moye** at La Route Orange, St Brelade, tel: 01534 747166 and **Royal Jersey Golf Club**, La Chemin au Grèves, Grouville, tel: 01534 854416. Anyone can play at the 18-hole courses at **Les Mielles**, St Ouen's Bay, tel: 01534 482787 or **Les Ormes Leisure Village**, St Brelade, tel: 01534 497000, or the 9-hole courses at Wheatlands, off Le Vieux Beaumont, St Peter, tel: 01534 888877 or Jersey Recreation Grounds, St Clement, tel: 01534 721938.

OTHER ACTIVITIES

Spas, Health and Leisure

For an island traditionally associated with old fashioned sea-side holidays, Jersey has certainly made a splash when it comes to spas. In St Helier alone there are four hotels with state-of-the-art spas where you can choose from a range of treatments, use the indoor pools and high-tech gyms. At the **Spa Sirène** in the Royal Yacht Hotel you can unwind with a steam mud rasul, a hydrotherapy bath, a sauna, or in the aromatherapy steam room, and chill out in the indoor vitality pool or under ice-cold bucket showers. (Note, though, that you need to be feeling flush to get in – those who are not hotel residents must spend at least £75 on treatments.) Hotel de France's **Ayush Wellness Spa** is based on ancient Hindu health and healing principles, while the chic **Club Hotel** has a swish spa that offers all kinds of feelgood treatments. The latest spa to open is the two-storey luxury **Grand Spa** at the born-again Grand Jersey Hotel, where guests and residents are pampered in six treatment rooms.

For a cheaper health option to the hotel spas try **Fitness First** at St Helier's

Playing at the Royal Jersey Golf Club, Grouville

Walks and Strolls

The North Coast is the best place for walking. The **North Coast Footpath** runs for 15 miles (24km) from **Grosnez** to **Rozel**. Some sections are quite steep, particularly as the path climbs up from the bays, but there is nothing seriously challenging. The walk can either be done in its entirety over a very long day, or in separate shortish sections at a gentler pace. The scenery is best in spring when wild flowers are in full bloom and birds come ashore to nest. The path occasionally diverts from the coast, but the route is well signed. Getting there and back is best done by bus. No. 3 goes from St Helier to Rozel, No. 8 returns from Grosnez. One of the most spectacular stretches is Bonne Nuit to Bouley Bay (4 miles/2.5km) (served by No. 4 bus from St Helier). You could also walk west from Bonne Nuit to La Saline. Or take bus No. 8 to Plémont, walk 5 miles (8km) to Devil's Hole and return to St Helier on No. 7.

Walks in the southwest corner of the island afford some splendid coastal views. **Portelet Common** on the headland between Portelet Bay and Ouaisné Bay commands a stunning panorama over Ouaisné and St Brelade's Bay to the northwest, and over Portelet Bay to the east. **Noirmont Promontory** is not quite as scenic but provides pleasant clifftop strolls and historic interest in its German Occupation relics. A longer walk takes you all the way from **Ouaisné Bay** to **La Corbière** (you could also start at St Brelade's or Beauport). Features such as the island prison and desalination plant don't enhance the scenery and the track occasionally diverts inland, but most of this rugged cliff path is unspoilt, with superb sea views. The walk ends with the striking view of Corbière Lighthouse (see page 56). From **St Helier** to **St Aubin** the long seafront promenade makes an ideal leisurely stroll or cycle ride; from St Aubin you can continue to Corbière along the old railway route, now a peaceful cycle- and footpath through varied scenery, from red squirrel-inhabited woodland to gorse-clad heathland. It's a gentle climb of 4 miles (6.4km), and you can return to St Aubin or St Helier by bus No. 12.

Waterfront Centre (tel: 0844 5712883) with a gym, cardio theatre, spinning room, sauna, steam room and beauty room. The neighbouring **Aqua Splash** has an 80-ft (25-m) six-lane pool, and an outdoor pool with flumes and slides. **Les Quennevais Sports Centre** at Don Farm, St Brelade (tel: 01534 449880) has a swimming pool, fitness centre, squash courts, arena sports and sauna/steam room.

Walking

Jersey packs in plenty of walks, from gentle strolls along seafront promenades, or down leafy lanes through woodland valleys, to the more dramatic north coast cliffs. In addition to the footpaths there are 50 miles (80km) of Green Lanes, with a speed limit of 15 mph (24 kmph) giving priority to pedestrians, cyclists and horse riders.

The Jersey Tourism website has an excellent section on walking, with information on themed, escorted walks. These take place almost every day from April to September and themes cover all aspects of the island, including wildlife, local customs, maritime history, smuggling and the German Occupation. Tours are led by enthusiastic and knowledgeable guides and the fee for most of them is only £5.

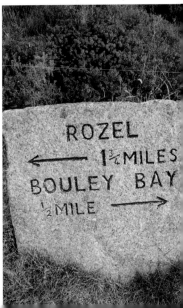

Destinations along the North Coast Footpath

More expensive, but well worth it, are the occasional 'Moon-walks', at low tide only, across the lunar-like landscape to Seymour Tower on the southeast coast. The tides can be treacherous here, and going alone is not advised. The Jersey Tourism website (www.jersey.com/walking) also has details of self-guided walks, with information on length and time, degree of difficulty, transport, attractions en route and re-freshment stops. Their free walking guide can be picked up at the tourist office or downloaded from the website.

Biking

Fit cyclists can forget the car on Jersey and use pedal power to enjoy the scenery. No distance is too far to cycle – though the hills can be strenuous and on occasions the local 4x4s leave you little space on the narrow country lanes. Cyclists should plan their routes around the 60-mile (96-km) sign-posted cycle network, including 50 miles (80km) of Green Lanes, which carry a 15mph (24kmph) speed limit for cars (usually but not always adhered to). Jersey Tourism provides a free map detailing cycling routes and the website (www.jersey.com/cycling) gives details for self-guided bike tours. One of the easiest and most attractive routes, suitable for families with small children, is the designated footpath/cycle ride following the old railway line from St Aubin to Corbière (*for bike hire, see page 117*).

ARTS AND ENTERTAINMENT

Most of the entertainment is focused on St Helier. **The Jersey Arts Centre**, Phillips Street, St Helier (tel: 01534 700444, www.artscentre.je) is a non-profit-making organi-sation that stages contemporary and classical concerts plus theatre and art exhibitions. Jersey's Edwardian **Opera House** (tel: 01534 511100, www.jerseyoperahouse.co.uk)

Masquerading at the Jersey Opera House

has been beautifully restored and hosts musical extravaganzas, concerts, drama, dance and very occasional operas.

Clubs

Nightlife focuses around the The Weighbridge, Liberation Square and the Waterfront Centre of St Helier, with high-decibel, late-night dives attracting a young crowd. For details of concerts, live bands or DJs, pick up a copy of the *Jersey Evening Post*.

Regarded by affluent young financiers as one of the coolest bars is **The Drift**, Royal Yacht Hotel, Liberation Square, a popular after-work rendezvous and a late-night bar offering a huge range of cocktails, drinks and snacks, live music or DJs. The nearby **Pure** nightclub at Caledonia Place has big name DJs at the weekend and funky dance music. A relative new nightspot is **La Cala** at 22 Beresford Street, which combines a bar, lounge, restaurant and nightclub, with DJs every night from 10pm, salsa classes on Tuesday, and a top-floor roof terrace during the summer months. On the Waterfront **The Bar Café** is a stylish bar where you can eat outside and enjoy views of Elizabeth Castle, while **Liquid** and **Envy** nightclubs offer a range of music from R'n'B and funky house to twisted disco.

For bars with music try **Chambers** on Mulcaster Street, which has live music (and disco) nightly from 11.30pm, or **Bar Rock** on The Waterfront, with musical hits from the 1950s to the early 1990s and themed nights (karaoke on Wednesday). Both bars are restricted to the over-18s and Bar Rock is for the over-20s only on Friday and Saturday.

Older visitors who remember Bergerac can head for the **Old Court House Inn** at St Aubin, which was the Royal Barge in the popular 1980s series.

SHOPPING

Jersey is not a full member of the EU, and VAT is non-existent. However, this doesn't mean that the shops are packed with bargains. Many of them put up prices for 'freight surcharge', then add to this the 3 percent Goods and Services tax (which came into effect in 2008), and the prices are around the same as those in the UK. Moreover, not all goods are VAT free – some shops retain VAT on goods that have come from the UK. The best buys are wines, spirits and tobacco, and to a lesser extent cosmetics, perfume and jewellery, which are all duty free. For customs restrictions that apply to luxury goods purchased in the Channel Islands *see page 121*.

The main shopping centre is St Helier, which has a pleasant pedestrianised High Street with the usual chainstores plus a large number of jewellers and shops selling cosmetics. As well as browsing here don't miss the indoor Central and Fish markets *(see page 33)*. Evening markets, selling arts and crafts and Jersey products, are held on alternate Thursdays from April to September at The Weighbridge.

Island Arts and Crafts

Some of the most popular shopping outlets are attached to the island's craft centres. At **Jersey Pottery** in Gorey Village *(see page 81)* you can watch potters throwing and painting in the factory and purchase ceramics (including seconds) and other gifts from the showroom. The pottery has been producing ceramics since 1946 and now exports all over the world, including to Harrods, Fortnum & Mason and Barney's of New York.

For jewellery you can try the shops in St Helier, or **Jersey Goldsmiths** at Lion Park, St Lawrence where you can purchase gold chains by the metre, watch the craftsmen,

Necklaces from Jersey Pearl

Vintages from La Mare
Wine Estates

commission a piece of jewellery – or just enjoy the landscaped gardens and lake. At **Jersey Pearl** you can have your own necklace made or choose from an extensive range of cultured, freshwater or simulated pearls. **Catherine Best**, based at The Windmill, Les Chenolles, St Peter, creates innovative pieces of jewellery, often from rare, fabulously coloured gemstones. For less expensive souvenirs try **Jersey Lavender** inland from St Brelade's Bay *(see page 54)*, where soaps, oils, colognes, creams and candles are made from the lavender essence.

The **Harbour Gallery** at Le Boulevard, St Aubin (daily 10.30am–5.30pm) is a large, well-run arts and crafts centre, with regularly changing contemporary exhibitions and some innovative paintings and textiles by local artists. Galleries here include the Jersey Silver Studio, Bead 'n' Crafts, Knit Wits (hand-dyed yarns) and Jersey Soap, which has unusual gifts including the Jersey walking stick, made from the stalks of the island's famous giant cabbages. For other Jersey specialities look for the red logo of Genuine Jersey, which promotes local produce. This covers crafts and jewellery as well as food and drink.

Locally made wines and spirits, black butter *(see page 105)*, jams and jellies can be found at **La Mare Wine Estates** in St Mary, which also has outlets in St Helier at the Spice House, the Central Market and at Maison La Mare in King Street.

CHILDREN'S JERSEY

For a traditional family holiday Jersey has the ideal ingredients: acres of sandy beaches, crab-filled rock pools, numerous sporting activities and a variety of family attractions. Top of the list should be **Durrell Wildlife** *(see page 71)*, whose gorillas, orang-utans, fruit bats and other endangered species will keep youngsters entertained (and educated) for at least half a day. Farmyard animals are one of the attractions at Hamptonne Country Life Museum *(see page 41)*. **Living Legend Village** (www.jerseyslivinglegend.co.je) is a firm favourite, with its lively, high-tech recreation of the history and traditions of the island, karting track, playground and adventure golf courses *(see page 40)*. In St Helier the **Maritime Museum** *(see page 34)* is full of hands-on exhibits, and the amphibious castle ferry to Elizabeth Castle *(see page 36)* makes an entertaining excursion. Young craft enthusiasts will enjoy watching the potters at work at **Jersey Pottery** in Gorey Village, and creating their own hand-painted piece of pottery at Glaze Craze. The **aMaizin! Maze and Adventure Park** (La Hougue Farm, St Peter, tel: 01534 482116, www.jerseyleisure.com) has a whole range of activities (gold panning, tractor rides and go-

Old-fashioned entertainment

karting among them) along with the maze itself, which opens in July and has a themed scavenger hunt with clues taking you through the labyrinth constructed entirely of maize. On the same site aMaizin! Craft opens during wet weather, providing arty, hands-on projects for all ages.

The best beach for youngsters is **St Brelade's Bay**, with its great swath of gently sloping sands and shallow waters, bucket-and-spade shops and child-friendly cafés. Children who are used to warm swimming pools may find the sea water on the cool side but it's never too cold for paddling or splashing around on the water's edge. The neighbouring **Ouaisné Bay** has some great rock pools at the far end where children can mess around fishing for shrimps, crabs and devil fish. Older children who are strong swimmers will love bodyboarding on the windswept bay of St Ouen's – or just sitting at a beachside café watching the stand-up surfers catching the Atlantic rollers. On a rainy day take children to **Aqua Splash** at St Helier's Waterfront Centre, which has an indoor pool with wave machine and bubble pool – plus an outdoor one with flumes and a tyre ride.

Fun among the rock pools at Ouaisné Bay

Jersey's latest attraction – ideal for adventure-seeking older children (and adults) – is the **Creepy Valley Activity Centr**e at Les Ormes Leisure Club, St Brelade (www.creepy valley.je). The attractive valley here is the setting for a range of exciting activities, from zip wires, aerial trekking and Powerfan freefall, jumping from a 40-ft (12-m) tower, to a military-style assault course and orienteering.

Calendar of Events

For a full listing of events go to www.jersey.com/events or pick up a current copy of the *What's On* guide for the events of the month.

February/March: Spring Specials: Over half the island's restaurants show off their new season cuisine and offer excellent value set-priced menus.

May: *Liberation Day* (9 May): celebrating the liberation from German Occupying forces. Gorey's *Fête de la Mer* (mid-May) with seafood stalls, alfresco dining and entertainment. *Spring Walking Week*: free guided walks for all ages. The late May *Foire de Jersey* is a traditional rural fair with food stalls, cattle and flower shows and entertainment. Also includes the Cheese Festival.

June: *June in Bloom* floral festival: a week in mid-June of open gardens, demonstrations, flower shows and walks. *Samarès Summer Festival* is held in the beautiful grounds of Samarès Manor.

July: *Bonne Nuit Harbour Festival*, in the third week: a day of activities for all ages with stalls, food and music.

August: *Battle of Flowers Carnival* (second Thursday in August): A highlight in the Jersey calendar, featuring a spectacular parade of flower-decked floats, musicians and entertainers. *Gorey Fête* in late August is a day of beach events, games, stalls, fairground rides and music.

September: *Jersey Live*, early September: billed as 'the biggest little indie rock festival in Europe', plus the *International Air Display*. During the *Autumn Walking Week* in mid-September you can take part in free coastal, country and historical walks, organised by Jersey Tourism.

October: Autumn events include the *Royal Jersey Horticultural Show* and *La Faîs'sie d'Cidre*, the lively Cider Festival at Hamptonne Country Life Museum.

October–November: Restaurants are packed out during the *Tennerfest*, six weeks (Oct–mid Nov) when you can have a meal for £10 at more than 100 restaurants.

EATING OUT

Eating out is an important part of life on the island and Jersey residents are spoilt for choice. A vast array of fabulously fresh seafood and fish is caught around the shores, and that's not the only local produce. Jersey produces its own vegetables, fruits, herbs, beef, pork and even cheeses. Not to mention the famous Jersey Royal potatoes and the creamy milk from Jersey cows.

Prosperous financiers and tax exiles ensure a year-round clientèle at up-market restaurants but at the other end of the spectrum there are plenty of more humble eateries, from country pubs, fish and chip outlets, beach cafés and kiosks. Seafood features in some capacity on virtually every menu. It might be a platter of lobster, scallops, crab and prawns, a succulent sea bass or bream, or just a tasty crab sandwich at a seaside kiosk.

Given the proximity to France, just 14 miles (22km) across the water from the east coast, it is not surprising that Gallic dishes feature on menus. Firm favourites are *moules à la crème* (with Jersey cream, of course), *moules frites* or *plateau de fruits de mer*. But generally speaking it is British cuisine that prevails. You never have to go far to find a fry-up breakfast, Sunday roast, scampi and chips, or pots of tea that you can take down to the beach.

Fresh crab claws

Where to Eat

For a tiny island Jersey has a remarkable number and variety of restaurants. You can choose from fashionable gastropubs, French restaurants, chic bistros, bustling trattorias, rustic inns and ethnic eateries. St Helier has the largest number of places to eat but Gorey and St Aubin both have highly rated restaurants, some with great views overlooking the sea. St Brelade's also has a good choice, from smart hotel dining to casual cafés virtually on the beach – a great spot for an early evening meal, watching the sun dip into the Atlantic.

Eating out at lunchtime, when many restaurants offer good-value two-course set menus, is often cheaper than evening dining. Hours are the same as those in the UK

The Boat House in St Aubin

at lunchtime, but evening meals tend to be served earlier, especially at seaside restaurants where last orders are often at 8 or 8.30pm or even earlier. In summer it's usually wise to reserve a table in advance, especially if it's a warm evening and you want to dine alfresco.

Shellfish

The clear, Gulf Stream-warmed waters around the island produce an abundance of shellfish including scallops, lobsters, chancre- or spider crabs, oysters and razor clams. The plump chancre crab is the most widely available but the sweeter spider crab is more sought after. Oysters, which used to thrive along the shores of the east coast, have seen a resurgence

Oysters ready for eating

through farming at Grouville. More than 4 million young oysters are now produced annually. The sweet and succulent 'Bouchot' mussels are also farmed in Gorey, grown from seed on wooden poles, but at the time of writing Jersey chefs were importing their mussels from Scotland as the ones produced locally were too small to dish up.

Ormers

If you happen to be on the beach from October to April during the neap tides, you might spot locals scouring the rocks at low tide in search of the near-mythical gastropod: the ormer. This indigenous mollusc, related to the abalone, is prized for its unique flavour and mother-of-pearl inner shell. The Channel Islands are the most northerly of its habitats and it was once a staple of island dinner tables. Traditionally the shellfish were carried home in a basket, soaked, shelled, scrubbed, beaten with a steak hammer, browned in a frying pan, then cooked in a casserole with belly of pork, shallots and carrots. Overfishing led to the ormer becoming a gourmet rarity, and nowadays there are stringent regulations to protect it. Fishing is only permitted between October and April, and only on the first day of each new or full moon and the five days following. Those who flout the rules are subject to hefty fines.

Fish

Among the fish that still inhabit Jersey waters – and which are most commonly seen on menus – are sea bass, bream, brill, conger, grey mullet, mackerel and sole. You'll also come across turbot, which is farmed in a German bunker on the east coast. The catch of the day is likely to vary daily and will probably be chalked up on a board. Local doesn't mean cheap, and if the fish is served by weight, check out what you're in for before giving the order. Jersey sea bass is becoming harder to find – a lot of what you see on menus is farmed in Spain, and it's not a patch on the line-caught bass fresh from Jersey waters.

Jersey Royals

First propagated in 1880 and traditionally fertilised by seaweed, Jersey Royal potatoes have earned worldwide acclaim not only for their waxy texture and earthy, nutty taste but the fact that they are ready well before the earliest crops of new potatoes in the UK. If you happen to be in Jersey in April, there is nothing to beat the very first crop of the season, straight from the soil, and served with Jersey butter and a sprinkling of parsley.

The acclaimed Jersey Royals

Jersey Royals are grown on the island's steeply sloping fields or *côtils*, and have never been grown outside the island. They are the only potato to be protected by a PDO (Protected Designation of Origin) under the Common Agricultural Policy of the European Union.

An abundance of fresh farm produce

Jersey Vegetables

Fresh, locally produced fruit and vegetables include strawberries, asparagus, broccoli, courgettes, peppers, tomatoes, and shitake mushrooms. You will see some of the produce when you are travelling round the island. Honesty boxes are left at the road side – you choose what you want and leave the correct change. Elsewhere, look for the Genuine Jersey Mark – the guarantee of local provenance. This applies to produce reared, grown and caught in Jersey, including dairy goods, fruit and vegetables, meat and poultry, fish, wines, ciders, spirits and beers.

Local Specialities

Before the days of Jersey Royals red and white beans were the island staples. They were grown on every farm on the island and it was the Jersey beans that inspired the Heinz baked variety – or so it's said. The beans were an essential ingredient of the hearty, cassoulet-like Jersey Bean Crock, cooked with pigs' trotters, belly of pork and onion. The café at Hamptonne Country Life Museum (see page 42) is one of the few places you can still find the Bean Crock (which is nowadays rather more refined than the original dish). It is served with cabbage loaf, a delicious doughy gold-crusted bread that is baked in large cabbage leaves. The bread can still be found in some bakeries. The Hamptonne café also makes *des Mèrvelles*, or Jersey Wonders, which taste like doughnuts (without the jam) and are shaped in a figure of eight. Jersey housewives traditionally cooked them as the tide went out. Occasionally you come across vraic buns, cakes made with yeast and raisins, and named after the vraic, or seaweed, which is collected from beaches and used as fertiliser. In days gone by families would gather to collect vraic from the beach, snacking on the buns (and swigging cider) between seaweed-collecting stints.

Black Butter

The unappetisingly named Jersey black butter, or *le nier beurre*, is not butter at all, but a type of apple preserve used to spread on bread or toast. Islanders made this in enormous quantities in the days when the cider industry was flourishing. Typically 700lb (318kg) of sliced apples, 20lb (9kg) of sugar, 24 lemons, spices and liquorice were added to a large

The Jersey Cow

Symbolic of the island, the Jersey cow is known for the richest milk in the world. The handsome tan and white doe-eyed cows feature as watermarks on Jersey bank notes – as well as on numerous souvenirs from milk jugs to tea towels. The purity of the breed has been guaranteed since 1789 when a ban was imposed on the import of live cattle to the island. Since the end of the 18th century it has been exported worldwide and there is still high demand. India, Japan, New Zealand, America and Fiji are just a few of the countries where the breed can be found. Jersey dairy products include butter, cream, yoghurt, organic milk, ice cream, crème fraîche and clotted cream, popular of course with Jersey cream teas. Those watching the waistline or cholesterol level can always opt for the fat-reduced or low-fat Jersey milk, which is widely available.

copper urn with 10 gallons (45l) of cider. The pot was stirred day and night, amid song, dance and general merriment, then poured into jars to last until the next black butter making session. The Jersey National Trust keeps the tradition alive and if you happen to be in Jersey in the latter part of October you can help out with peeling or stirring in the bakehouse at The Elms, La Cheve Rue, St Mary. Black butter can be bought at La Mare Vineyards or from Spice House in St Helier's Central Market.

Wine and Cider

Jersey is sunny and shares the same degree of latitude as the Champagne region, so it's only natural the island should make its own fizz. La Mare Wine Estate, St Mary produces Cuvée de la Mar, a sparking Brut wine made in the traditional *méthode champenoise*. Following the success of the Cuvée, La Mare is now producing a pink fizz called Lillie - after Jersey's Lilly Langtry. Still white and red wines, apple

Culinary Events

The island hosts a fast-growing number of foodie events, kicking off with the Spring Specials (mid-February to end March) when almost half the island's restaurants show off the best of their culinary skills and offer great-value set-price menus. The *Tennerfest* (October to mid November) is hugely popular, with great bargains to be had at more than 100 eateries (lunch or dinner from £10). At many fairs stalls sell everything from Jersey oysters to gourmet burgers. The Gorey *Fête de la Mer* in May is known for alfresco seafood dining, the *Foire de Jersey* features food stalls, French markets, and a *Cheese Festival*. October sees *Le Fais'sie d'Cidre* (Cider Festival), a lively event held at Hamptonne Country Life Museum to celebrate the island's heritage of apple cultivation and cider production.

brandy, liqueurs and a delicious French-style sparkling cider are also made at La Mare.

Cider was first introduced to the Channel Islands by the Normans and until relatively recently it was the main drink of the island. In the 17th century it was given by farmers to their staff to make up their wages. At the cider festival *(see previous page)* you can watch the old cider-making methods, with a horse crushing the apples and the juice extracted on the twin-screw press. Nowadays a pint of beer is far more popular than a glass of cider. Jersey Brewery has been brewing since 1871, although it moved from old premises in Ann Street in 2004 to a new micro-brewery at Longueville in St Saviour. Up to 5,000 barrels of award-winning beer are produced annually. Jersey Best is a 3.6 percent ABV dark beer with a distinctive hop flavour, while Jersey Special is a 4.5 percent lighter coloured, slightly sweeter beer.

Mary Ann Bitter, brewed in Jersey

PLACES TO EAT

The price bands are based either on a three-course evening meal for one, or for lunch or tea where no evening meal is served. Prices exclude drinks and service charge, but are inclusive of the 3 percent Goods & Services Tax:

££££ over £40   **££** £15–25
£££ £25–40   **£** under £15

ST HELIER

Bistro Central ££££ *7–11 Don Street, tel: 01534 876933, www.bistro-central.com.* Appealing Parisian-style bistro in the heart of St Helier offering a full *à la carte* menu, *plats du jour*, set menus, or, from 2.15–5pm, a café menu featuring soup, snails, omelettes or fish. For seafood lovers the *assiette de fruits de mer* is an irrisistible platter of oysters, crab claws, lobster, whelks and winkles. Closed Sun.

Bohemia ££££ *Green Street, tel: 01534 880588, www.bohemia jersey.com.* Jersey's top gourmet restaurant under head chef Shaun Rankin, within the chic contemporary surrounds of the Club Hotel and Spa. Dishes feature Jersey ingredients where possible, whether its three-hour cooked duck eggs with shiitake mushrooms and asparagus, pancetta-wrapped local scallops or Jersey lobster and crab.

Cafe Zephyr ££–£££ *The Royal Yacht Hotel, Weighbridge, tel: 01534 720511, www.theroyalyacht.com.* Buzzing brasserie where fashionistas come to see and be seen. It is open from 9am until 1am, starting with an imaginative breakfast menu and serving a range of dishes throughout the day, from sushi and sashimi to the Royal Yacht Burger.

Colomberie Sushi and Noodle Bar £ *La Colomberie, tel: 01534 876005.* Part of the ever-expanding Jersey Pottery emporium, the café serves sandwiches, salads, cakes and pastries with a selection of hot noodles, stir fries and curries to eat in or takeaway. Internet access and Wifi hotspot.

Le Dicq Shack £ *Dicq Slipway, Dicq Road, no phone.* Bring your own bottle and chill on the sands with tasty freshly cooked Thai cuisine. Try red snapper stir fry with lemon and ginger, Thai curry or plum and lemon ginger ribs.

Green Olive ££ *1 Anley Street, tel: 01534 728198.* Renowned for creating mouthwatering menus from local produce, the Green Olive specialises in vegetables, seafood and poultry. All the food here is freshly prepared. Closed Mon and Sun, and Sun lunch .

The Lamplighter £ *9 Mulcaster Street, tel: 01534 723119.* CAMRA pub of 2008, the Lamplighter is renowned for its real ales, with four direct from the cask. This is a traditional town pub with wooden beams and working gas lamps. Snacks and soup are served at scrubbed pine tables. Lunch time only.

Museum Brasserie ££–£££ *Jersey Museum, The Weighbridge, tel: 01523 510069.* This central brasserie is very popular with locals for its pretty alfresco area, freshly caught seafood, pastas and salads. Brunches are served at weekends and from Wednesday to Saturday evening music and cocktails draw the crowds. Closed dinner Mon–Tue, and Sun off-season.

Olive Branch ££ *41 La Colomberie, tel: 01534 615993.* A stylish spot for an Italian meal, whether for home-made pasta, meat, fish, vegetarian dishes or one of the delicious pizzas cooked in a wood-burning oven. Closed Sun.

AROUND THE ISLAND

BONNE NUIT

Bonne Nuit Beach Café £–££ *Bonne Nuit Beach, tel: 01534 861656.* Inviting beach café with lovely views of the fishing harbour. Come for full English breakfasts, light lunches, seafood specials, crab sandwiches or cream teas. There is also a Thai menu, available for takeaway. Local fishermen bring in the catch of the day and all food is freshly cooked to order. Lunch only (but you can get evening Thai takeaways).

BOULEY BAY

Black Dog Bar ££ *tel: 01534 869129*. Named after the fictitious monster dog that roamed the north coast, this pub has plenty of character and excellent food. Popular all year round, with log fires in winter.

GOREY

Bass and Lobster Foodhouse £££ *Gorey Coast Road, tel: 01534 859590, www.bassandlobster.com*. Previously called The Gorey Village, the restaurant was taken over by well-known Jersey chef, Roger White in 2009, and completely revamped. You can be assured of locally sourced seafood here including hand-dived scallops and line-caught sea bass. Don't miss the signature dish for the new restaurant: grilled fillet of local sea bass with creamy lobster risotto and shellfish sauce. Despite the name of the restaurant there is always a choice of meat on the menu – again, mainly locally sourced. Closed Sun, and Mon lunch.

Castle Green Gastropub ££ *La Route de la Côte, tel: 01534 840218*. A popular Gorey eatery with great views of the castle and creative cuisine. Come for a light lunch or leisurely dinner and expect sushi and sashimi, hand-dived scallops, roast rib-eye steak and the catch of the day. There is an unusually good choice of wines, many served by the glass. Closed Sun pm and Mon.

Suma's £££ *Gorey Hill, tel: 01534 853291*. The little sister of Longueville Manor *(see page 114)*, Suma's is a small, stylish restaurant serving innovative English cuisine with a Mediterranean twist. The dining room is bright and modern but the sought-after seats in summer are those on the terrace with outstanding views of Grouville Bay and Mont Orgueil Castle. Dishes are artfully presented and full of flavour. Choose from the *à la carte* menu, the cheaper early supper or lunch menus, or – if you're up in time – Suma's big Saturday breakfast (9.30–10.30am).

Village Bistro £££ *Gorey Village, tel: 01534 853429*. In Gorey Village, as opposed to the more characterful harbour, the bistro is popular for its friendly, laid-back atmosphere and excellent value contemporary cuisine. Seafood predominates but there are also plenty of steak, lamb, duck and chicken dishes. Closed Mon.

GRÈVE DE LECQ

Moulin de Lecq ££ *tel: 01534 482818.* An ancient water mill with a stream that flows into the sea. The tavern retains original stone and wood features and the main bar is built around the watermill's cog wheels and gearing mechanisms. The newly built restaurant is comparatively characterless but you can eat in the garden in summer.

ROZEL

The Hungry Man £ *Rozel Bay, tel: 01534 863227.* Kiosk on the waterside, famous for its delicious crab sandwiches. You can sit at port-side tables with views of the bay, and walk along the pier for views of France on a clear day. Open daily 9.30am–4.30pm.

The Navigator £££ *La Breque du Nord, Rozel Harbour, tel: 01534 861444, www.navigatorrestaurant.co.uk.* Come for seafood cataplana, grilled sardines, tiger prawns or linguini lobster, and enjoy fabulous harbour views from the floor to ceiling windows. For the special Navigator seafood platter order 12 hours in advance.

ST AUBIN

The Boat House ££–£££ *1 North Quay, tel: 01534 744226 (Sails Brasserie) and 01534 747141 (Quay Bar), www.jerseyboathouse.com.* Built on the site of a former boatyard, this modern glass and timber building overlooks the port. In the first-floor Sails Brasserie fish choices include scallops and oysters, sea bass, sea bream and sole, while the more informal Quay Bar on the ground floor has a cheaper menu with mussels and chips, steak or burgers. Sails Brasserie: dinner only Mon–Thur and Sat, lunch only Sun; Quay Bar: Nov–Mar closed Sun evening.

Danny's Restaurant £££ *St Aubin Harbour, tel: 01534 747306, www.dannys.je.* Energetic and charismatic chef Danny Moisan enjoys producing dishes with a difference, such as scallops with pineapple and his 'secret Asian dressing', or vanilla red snapper with smoky baba ghanouj and rocket pesto over garlic mash. This is a new fashionable restaurant with a leafy courtyard and a laid-back atmosphere. Closed Mon.

Salty Dog Bar and Bistro £££ *Le Boulevard, tel: 01534 742760; www.saltydogbistro.com.* Fashionable, laid-back eatery with warm, oriental decor, cocktail bar and fusion cuisine. A Thai fish Tom Yam soup or twice cooked goats' cheese soufflé might be followed by the sumptuous Surf and Turf (lobster, scallops and king prawns with prime beef fillet in a chilli, garlic and coriander sauce), then Jersey black butter and banana pudding with toffee sauce and ice cream. Very popular – be sure to book.

ST BRELADE'S AND OUAISNÉ BAY

The Beach House ££–£££ *Ouaisné Bay, tel: 01534 498605.* Fabulous bay views and friendly service compensate for sosmewhat mediocre cuisine at Jersey's newest restaurant. International menu, with a long list of tapas for starters. Open for meals and drinks all day from noon, and breakfast at weekends.

Crab Shack £–££ *St Brelade's Bay, tel: 01534 744611.* A casual, all-day eatery with a terrace right on the bay. There are fry-up breakfasts, fish and chips, BBQ ribs and Jersey chancre crab, which comes with a shell-cracking wooden mallet. Open all day and fully licensed; last orders Tue–Thur 8pm, Fri–Sat 8.30pm, Mon 5pm.

Ocean Restaurant ££££ *Atlantic Hotel, Le Mont de la Pulente, tel: 01534 744101.* Dine in style in one of Jersey's top-end restaurants with breathtaking views over St Ouen's Bay. The Michelin-starred hotel restaurant is renowned for classic British cuisine with a modern twist – scallop and apple, rabbit fillet with rhubarb confit, red mullet with local peppers, duck *foie gras* and red mullet cappuccino. Head chef Mark Jordan uses the finest and freshest from Jersey's coast and countryside.

Oyster Box £££–££££ *St Brelade's Bay, tel: 01534 743311, www.oysterbox.co.uk.* A stylish restaurant right on the bay where you can pop in between ocean dips or beach games for a beef burger or gourmet sandwich or linger over a sumptuous platter of *fruits de mer*. Excellent choice of seafood including sushi and sashimi, Thai tempura king prawns, oysters with hot garlic butter and chorizo and whole chancre crab. The setting is contemporary, with fishy decor and alfresco terrace tables. Closed Mon lunch and Sun supper.

Old Smugglers Inn £–££ *Ouaisné Bay, tel: 01534 741510.* Converted 17th-century cottages with real ales, log fires and a good range of pub food.

Old Portelet Inn £–££ *Portelet, St Brelade, tel: 01534 741899.* Huge family pub in an old farmhouse, with a bar, bistro and lovely views of Portelet Bay. Play areas inside and out, live entertainment most evenings, piped music.

Pizza Express £–££ *St Brelade's Bay, tel: 01534 499049.* The pizzas here are enhanced by the panoramic views from the huge picture windows.

Wayside Cafe £–££ *St Brelade's Bay, no booking.* One of Jersey's most popular beachside cafés – don't be surprised if you have to queue. Apart from a great location right on the island's most scenic beach it serves excellent breakfasts, steaks, burgers, Thai crispy duck salad and sea bass on Spanish paella. Also home-made cakes and puddings.

Zanzibar £££ *St Brelade's Bay, tel: 01534 741081.* Quirky restaurant with African decor and eclectic menu. Outdoor eating with fine sea views. Closed Mon.

ST CLEMENT

Green Island Restaurant £££ *Green Island, tel: 01534 857787.* The southernmost restaurant in the UK, Green Island has great sea views and outstanding seafood. The terrace overlooks Green

Island, whose sandy beaches draw hordes of beach lovers in summer. There is a casual beach café atmosphere and a long list of locally sourced fish such as lobster, langoustines, scallops, sand eels and sea bass. Closed all day Mon and Sun pm.

ST LAWRENCE

Bistro Soleil ££ *La Route de la Haule, Beaumont, tel: 01534 720249.* Light and airy beach-side bistro attracting a fashionable, casual crowd for the fine views and platters of lobster, crab and fresh fish. The bistro is at its best on a sunny day when you can dine alfresco under parasols. Good value set menus. Closed Mon, and Sun pm.

Hamptonne Café ££ *Hamptonne Country Life Museum, La Rue de la Patente; tel: 01534 863955.* Try the sweet and savoury island specialities, such as the doughnut-like Jersey Wonders or Beancrock with cabbage loaf, washed down with Jersey cider. Picnic hampers can be prepared for lunch in the orchard, and there are delicious cream teas and home-made cakes. Open daily 10am–4.45pm only.

ST OUEN'S

Big Vern's ££ *La Grande Route des Mielles, tel: 01534 481705.* Surfers love this long-established beach café for its eggs and bacon, scampi and chips, burgers or seafood. You can sit outside at wooden tables and watch the pros ride the rollers. All-day breakfast is a speciality and there are early evening sunset specials from 6pm; last orders in summer 8.30pm.

ST SAVIOUR

Longueville Manor ££££ *Longueville Road, tel: 01534 725501, www.longuevillemanor.com.* A country house hotel with a long-standing reputation for gastronomy. Meals are served in the elegant wood-panelled Oak Room or the bright and airy Garden Room. Cuisine is contemporary English/French, with the emphasis on Jersey ingredients (vegetables, fruit and herbs are grown in the kitchen garden). Impeccable service; fine wine list.

A–Z TRAVEL TIPS

A Summary of Practical Information

A

ACCOMMODATION

Hotel accommodation ranges from bed and breakfasts to chic boutique or country house hotels. Several of the top hotels have undergone multimillion-pound refurbishments in the last three years, and a quarter of the hotel guest rooms are now within the four- and five-star range. Budget hotels, however, are hard to come by, and self-catering is limited.

If you are going in July and August it is wise to book well in advance, especially if you require a room with a view. At other times of year there is little problem. Many hotels are closed from November to February. Contact Jersey Tourism (tel: 01534 448888, www.jersey.com) for a copy of their excellent 'Stay Jersey' brochure or access a list of accommodation from their website. JerseyLink (same contact details) is their official accommodation booking service for hotels, guesthouses and self-catering. This allows you to view current information on availability, prices and special offers. No charge is made for the service. Most establishments will require a deposit or credit card details before confirming a reservation. A large number of hotels have special offers, such as three nights for the price of two or free car hire with three or more nights stay. Booking online at some hotels can save you 10 percent.

Specialist travel agents for Jersey who can organise tailor-made holidays with travel, transfers, insurance and car hire, include the Channel Islands Travel Service (tel: 01534 496699, www.jersey travel.com/sj) and Channel Islands Direct (tel: 08444 937495, www.channelislandsdirect.co.uk). Condor Ferries (tel: 0845 230 1430, www.condorbreaks.com) can organise accommodation if you are taking a car across on a Condor Ferry from Weymouth, Poole or Portsmouth.

For **self-catering** contact Macoles Self Catering (tel: 01534 488100, www.macoles.com) who have details of over 90 percent of the island's self-catering units. Or, for a holiday with a difference, you can stay at one of the beautifully sited fortresses. observation towers and follies that have been restored by Jersey Heritage (www.jerseyheritage.org) as self-catering accommodation. They include the red-and-white striped Archirondel Tower near St Catherine's Breakwater *(see page 76)*, the Barge Aground folly at St Ouen's, the German Radio Tower overlooking the Corbière Lighthouse *(see page 57)*, the Seymour Tower *(see page 83)* and La Crête Fort and Fort Leicester, both on the North Coast *(see pages 68–9)*.

Many visitors base themselves in St Helier, which has a good bus service to all parts of the island and is the starting point for island bus and boat tours. However, some of the smaller centres such as St Aubin, Gorey or St Brelade's Bay are far more picturesque, and have some excellent restaurants and good transport links.

AIRPORT

Located in St Peter, 5 miles (8km) west of St Helier, the airport is small by UK standards but equipped with exchange facilities, ATMs, food outlets and shops. For flight information tel: 01534 446000 or visit www.jerseyairport.com. The Departures Lounge was revamped in 2009 with new Duty Free shop, restaurant and facilities. Hire cars can be picked up in the Arrivals Hall. A taxi from the airport to St Helier costs from £13 to £16 depending on the location of your hotel. Bus No. 15 operates roughly every 30 minutes in summer to St Helier via Red Houses and St Aubin. For timetables check Connex Transport (www.mybus.je). Tickets (£1.50 adults, £1 children and students) can be bought on the bus.

B

BICYCLE HIRE

For the energetic and eco-friendly there is a 96-mile (155-km) network of well-marked cycle routes, including Green Lanes where the speed limit is 15 mph (24kmph). Visitors who prefer to plan their own routes can consult the Jersey Tourism website www.jersey. com/cycling. A cycling guide and map can be picked up from the Jersey Tourism Visitor Centre in St Helier.

In St Helier you can hire bikes from Aardvar/Zebra Hire (9 The Esplanade and 10 Commercial Street, tel: 01534 736556, www. zebrahire.com). Adult and child mountain bikes, tandems, touring bikes and trailers are all available and a free puncture/breakdown service is offered island-wide. In St Aubin Jersey Cycle Tours (Old German Tunnels, Railway Path, St Aubin, tel: 01534 746780, www. jerseycyletours.com) will help with your choice of hybrid bikes, tag-alongs and baby carriages, and will refund days lost if you have bad weather and have hired for several days. They also operate Funbikes (www.funbikes.com) for cycling along the promenade between St Helier and St Aubin – a safe and scenic route for families.

Visitors coming to the island on Condor Ferries can bring bikes to the island free of charge.

BUDGETING FOR YOUR TRIP

Petrol is about 10 percent cheaper than in the UK; a pint of beer or lager the same as the UK; a bottle of house wine £12–£16; soft drink £1.20, cup of coffee £1.50–£2; cycle hire from £10 per day or £35 a week, car hire from £35 per day or £135 a week. Bus fares £1 or £1.50; one-day bus pass £6 (family £14), three-day bus pass £15 (family £36). Whole day island bus tour: £15

Most attractions are free for young children and substantial reductions are given to senior citizens and students. The Jersey Pass (www.jerseypass.com) can save you money if you intend to spend a fair amount of time sightseeing. It is an all-inclusive ticket for two, four or six consecutive days, allowing entry to 11 of the island's leading attractions. The pass comes with a free guide-book and can be booked online or picked up at Jersey Tourism Visitor Centre.

C

CAMPING

The island's campsites are open during the summer season only. Since there are only four sites space is restricted and reservations are advisable. The best sites are Beuvelande (tel: 01534 852223, www. jerseycamping.com) and Rozel Camping Park (tel: 01534 855200, www.rozelcamping. co.uk) which has views of France from one of its four fields and is within walking distance of the pretty harbour of Rozel, renowned for good restaurants. Rose Farm Campsite (tel: 01534 741231, www.jerseycamping.com) is a large site 10 minutes' walk from St Brelade's Bay. All the sites have heated swimming pools. Camping off-site is against the law and it is forbidden to pitch a tent anywhere on the island except on a designated site.

CAR HIRE

Car hire is cheaper than in the UK and petrol prices about 10 percent less. The minimum legal age to hire a car is 20 and there are varying maximum age restrictions. A valid driving licence is required, with no endorsements for dangerous or drunken driving in the last five years. Car hire companies are plentiful and there is little difference in price between the international and local companies. Hire firms include:

Avis (tel: freephone 0800 7351110, www.avisjersey.co.uk)

Europcar (tel: 0800 735 0735, www.europcarjersey.com/wts)

Hertz Rent-A-Car (tel: 01534 636666, www.hertzci.com)

Falles Hire Cars Ltd (tel: 01534 495000, www.fallesjersey.co.uk)

Zebra Hire (tel: 01534 736556, www.zebrahire.com)

All rented cars are branded with a large letter H on the number plate.

CLIMATE AND TIDE

Jersey has the highest average number of sunshine hours in the British Isles, although the summer temperatures are no higher than those in some parts of southern England. In the summer months the island has a daily average of eight hours of sunshine and an aveage maximum temperature of 68°F (20°C). As in the UK, the best months to go are from May to September, the hottest months being July and August. High temperatures in mid-summer are tempered by sea breezes. The following chart gives the average maximum temperature for St Helier.

	J	F	M	A	M	J	J	A	S	O	N	D
°C	9	8	11	13	16	19	21	21	19	16	12	10
°F	48	46	52	55	61	66	70	70	66	61	54	50

The sea temperatures are refreshing for swimming, averaging 62.8°F (17.1°C) in summer. The island has one of the largest tidal movements in the world. During spring tides Jersey's surface area increases from 45 to 63 sq miles (72 to 100 sq km) and the vertical difference between high and low water can be as much as 40ft (12 metres).

CLOTHING

The climate is similar to that of the southern part of the UK and the average temperature only a couple of degrees warmer, so take a couple of sweaters and rainproofs even in summer. Otherwise T-shirts and shorts/skirts should suffice, not forgetting a sunhat, sunglasses and suncream – the sun's rays can be deceptively strong. Casual wear is accepted in all but top-end hotels and restaurants where more formal wear would be expected. Some of the St Helier nightclubs refuse entry to anyone in jeans and trainers. On beaches the law requires that people 'do not act in a manner reasonably likely to offend public decency'. Topless bathing is generally accepted, though not widespread, and baring all on the island is inappropriate. Shopping in a swimsuit in St Helier is best avoided, too.

CRIME AND SAFETY

Jersey is a safe place for a holiday but it is worth taking all the usual precautions: always lock car doors and don't leave your valuables unattended. Dial 999 for police, fire, ambulance or coastal rescue services. Report a loss or theft to the police within 24 hours if an insurance claim is to be made.

CUSTOMS AND ENTRY REQUIREMENTS

Jersey has the same passport and visa requirements as the UK. Although a passport is therefore not necessary for visitors arriving from the UK, airline passengers will need valid photographic ID in order to travel, and a passport is required for trips to France. Other EU citizens require ID cards. Citizens from Australia, Canada, New Zealand, and the US need a valid passport but no visa; those from South Africa now require a visa.

As Jersey is not a full member of the European Union, you can still purchase duty-free items when travelling to and from the island. Maximum allowances are: 200 cigarettes or 100 cigarillos or 50 cigars or 350 grams of tobacco; 1 litre of spirits or 4 litres of sparkling or fortified wines and 4 litres of other wines. 60cl/ml perfume; 250 cc/ml eau de toilette; £340-worth of other goods (watches, jewellery, cameras, etc).

D

DRIVING

Jersey has the highest ratio of cars to people of anywhere in Europe, and around 36 percent of car trips on the island are less than 2 miles (3km). St Helier is notorious for traffic jams. Elsewhere driving is relatively stress-free, but beware of the very narrow lanes in the countryside, many of which are used by tractors, cyclists and pedestrians. Given these narrow lanes and the maximum speed limit of 40 mph (64kmph) there is no point in bringing or hiring a high performance car – although a remarkable number of islanders seem to own them. Despite its small size the island has more than 350 miles (563km) of paved roads. You may lose your way in the rural interior but it won't be for long. Signposting is reasonably good and you are never very far from a village or beach resort.

Visitors bringing their own car to Jersey on Condor Ferries (www.condorferries.com) must have an insurance certificate or International Green Card, a vehicle registration document, valid driving licence or International Driving Permit (UK Internationalal Driving Permits are not valid).

Rules of the Road. Rules reflect those of the UK: Driving is on the left; seat belts are compulsory for adult front seat passengers, children must wear belts or a suitable child/infant restraint in both front and rear seats; it is an offence to hold a mobile phone while driving. Fixed alcohol limits and road-side breath testing are similar to the UK. Penalties are severe, with up to a £2,000 fine or 6 months' imprisonment for the first offence plus unlimited driving licence disqualification.

The maximum speed limit on the island is 40 mph (64kmph), reduced to 30 mph (50 kmph) or 20 mph (32 kmph) in built-up areas and 15 mph (24 kmph) on Green Lanes where priority is given to pedestrians, horses and cyclists. Yellow lines across roads at intersections indicate 'Stop and give way'. A single yellow line along the length of the kerb means parking is prohibited day or night, and is liable to a fine. The 'Filter in Turn' system, whereby vehicles from each direction take it in turn to cross or join the traffic from other directions, is used at some of the main junctions. Traffic lights in Jersey change from red to green with no amber in between.

Parking. Parking requires the pre-purchase of paycards or 'scratchcards'. These are available from Jersey Tourism, hire car companies, post offices, garages, shops, Condor Ferries or anywhere displaying the paycard logo (a blue P inside a red C), but annoyingly not in the actual car parks that you need them for – Sand Street is the only exception. The cards are available as individual units or in books of 10 and are required from Monday to Saturday 8am–5pm (Bank Holidays excepted) in car parks with the paycard logo and on-street parking in the red and yellow zones. You scratch off the day, date, month, hour and minutes on the card to show time of arrival, and leave it on the dashboard. When using more than one single-unit paycard, you scratch off the following cards identically. The charge for parking 'on-street' is one unit per stay. You are allowed to stay for 20 minutes in the yellow zone, 60 minutes in the red. The cards are not required at the harbour, airport and waterfront car parks, where a pay-on-exit scheme is operated.

E

ELECTRICITY

The current is the same as that of the UK, 240 volts AC, with British-style three-pin sockets. Visitors from other European countries will need an adapter; those from the US also need a tranformer.

EMBASSIES AND HIGH COMMISSIONS

Australia Australian High Commission, Australia House, The Strand, London WC2B 4LA; tel: 020 7379 4334, www.uk.embassy.gov.au.

Canada Canada High Commission, 1 Grosvenor Square, London W1K 4AB; tel: 020 7258 6600, www.unitedkingdom.gc.ca.

New Zealand New Zealand High Commission, New Zealand House, 80 Haymarket, London SW1Y 4TQ; tel: 020 7930 8422, www.nzembassy.com.

Republic of Ireland Irish Embassy, 17 Grosvenor Place, London SW1X 7HR; tel: 020 7235 2171, www.embassyofireland.co.uk.

South Africa South Africa High Commission, South Africa House, Trafalgar Square, London WC2N 5DP; tel: 020 7451 7299, www.southafricahouse.com.

United States American Embassy, 24 Grosvenor Square, London W1A 1AE; tel: 020 7499 9000, www.usembassy.org.uk.

EMERGENCIES

In an emergency, dial 999 for police, fire, ambulance or sea rescue.

G

GAY AND LESBIAN TRAVELLERS

Jersey is more conservative than the UK. The age of consent for men is still 18 and Civil Partnerships are not recognised on the island, though they are currently under discussion. However a small and friendly gay scene exists on the island and the general attitude of islanders towards gays is not so different from that in the UK. One of the very few specifically gay venues is the new Vada in St Helier.

GETTING TO JERSEY

Jersey Tourism provides comprehensive information on air and ferry services from the UK. Year-round package holidays, either by sea or air for short or longer breaks, can be arranged through British tour operators. Specialist operators include Channel Islands Travel Services (tel: 01534 496600, www.jerseytravel.com) and Discover Jersey (tel: 0844 415 6653, www.discoverjersey.com). Alternatively most of the hotels, guesthouses and self-catering establishments on the island can arrange travel for you, as well as travel insurance and car rental if necessary.

By Air

Direct flights operate to Jersey from around 30 UK airports. The majority of flights are operated by Flybe (tel: 0871 700 2000, www.flybe.com), who fly from Gatwick, Heathrow, Birmingham, Manchester, Newcastle, Doncaster, Leeds, Bradford, Southend, Southampton, Bristol, Exeter, Dublin, Cardiff, Edinburgh, Glasgow, Aberdeen, Inverness, Dundee and the Isle of Man. Some flights only operate during the summer season. British Airways (tel: 0870 850 9850, www.ba.com), flies from Gatwick. The Guernsey-based airline, Aurigny (tel: 01481 822886, www.aurigny.com) has a direct service between London Stansted and Jersey. Low cost carriers have brought down prices of flights to Jersey but airport charges are high and there are few real bargains. When booking, watch out for all the hidden extras. With Flybe, for example, what is advertised as a £10 (one-way) flight is almost £100 by the time you have added taxes, airport charges and luggage. Prices vary considerably according to the time of year. Cheapest fares are normally secured by booking well in advance through the airline website and by avoiding high season and weekends.

Aurigny *(see details above)* and Blue Islands (tel: 0845 620 2122, www.blueislands.com) provide a channel-hopping service between Jersey, Alderney and Guernsey.

By Sea

Condor Ferries (tel: 0870 243 5100, www.condorferries.com) operates fast, state-of-the-art ferries to Jersey from Poole and Weymouth from April to October and from Weymouth only in winter. In high season there are up to four crossings a day, in winter just the one morning crossing from Weymouth. The services takes around three hours if you go on a ferry direct to Jersey, four if it stops at Guernsey en route. The wave-piercing catamarans all take cars and provide comfortable seating, duty-free shops with some excellent deals, a bar and café, and play area for children. The open deck affords spectacular views of Jersey as you arrive. Crossings can be rough and in bad weather ferries are occasionally cancelled. Condor also operates a year-round (Mon–Sat) traditional ferry which takes about 10 hours.

Inter-Island Ferries and France

Condor *(see above)* operates a high-speed car ferry service between St Malo and Jersey (2 hours 30 mins) and between Guernsey and Jersey. Manches Iles Express (tel: 01534 880756, www.manche-iles-express.com) links Jersey with Guernsey and Sark, and has services from St Helier to Granville and Carteret in Normandy and from Gorey to Carteret (passport required).

GUIDES AND TOURS

Tantivy Blue Coach Tours (tel: 01534 706706, www.jerseycoaches.com) is a long-established, reasonably-priced coach and tour operator offering all-day, morning and evening tours, covering the coast and popular island attractions. There are themed visits, such as Farms and Gardens, individual sites (eg Durrell Wildlife or Jersey War Tunnels) and an evening's entertainment in St Aubin. Minibus Direct (tel: 01534 853287, www.jerseyminibus.com) specialises in excursions, tours, nights out, and airport and harbour transfers.

H

HEALTH AND MEDICAL CARE

The UK has ended its reciprocal arrangement entitling UK visitors to free health care in Jersey and, apart from treatment solely within Jersey's A&E department, visitors have to pay for medical services and treatment. This includes emergency hospital treatment (such as operations) not within A&E, repatriation, out-patient appointments, GP visits and prescriptions. UK visitors are therefore advised to take out comprehensive health insurance or check that their existing policy covers travel to the island. Australia, New Zealand and France have reciprocal care agreements with Jersey which cover emergency hospital treatment.

The General Hospital at Gloucester Street, St Helier (tel: 01534 442000) has a 24-hour emergency unit. The majority of GP surgeries provide a service for visitors. Jersey Tourism can provide a leaflet with the details of island surgeries; alternatively ask your hotel or consult the yellow pages of the telephone directory. Medical prescriptions can be dispensed at any of the island pharmacies.

HOLIDAYS

Jersey has the same public holidays as the UK with an additional day's holiday on 9 May, Liberation Day, commemorating the end of the German Occupation in 1945.

1 January	New Year's Day
March or April	Good Friday and Easter Monday
First and last Mon in May	Spring Bank Holidays
9 May	Liberation Day
Last Monday in August	August Bank Holiday
25 December	Christmas Day
26 December	Boxing Day

L

LANGUAGE

English is spoken throughout the island but has only been the official language since the 1960s. The island's tradition is French, and even today some French words are used by the court and legal professions. In St Helier and other parts of the island you will see some street names in French, occasionally with the contemporary English names alongside. On rare occasions you can overhear some of the older residents speaking in Jèrriais, the local patois based on Norman French. Until World War II this dialect was widely spoken, with true French used to conduct written business. Local societies are anxious to keep the historic dialect alive; there are regular pieces in Jèrriais in the *Jersey Evening Post* and the language is taught in some schools.

M

MAPS

At Jersey Tourism you can pick up the free Island Visitor Map showing attractions, sports facilities and cycle routes. A map of St Helier is also included. Free maps are also available from the bus station and most hotels. Should you require something more detailed you can purchase the 1:19,000 Jersey Street Atlas or the Perry's Guide in booklet form, which details every little lane. If you are walking your way around the island you might consider the Ordnance Survey style Jersey Official Leisure Map.

MEDIA

All English national newspapers and many foreign ones arrive in the early morning, weather permitting. The *Jersey Evening Post*, the island's Monday to Saturday newspaper, gives you a good idea of Jersey life, especially politics and gossip, and has useful practical information including times of the tides and what's on. The free monthly *What's On* brochure, which you can pick up on arrival, or from Jersey Tourism, is packed with information on attractions and activities, including guided walks, beaches, entertainment and eating out. All national UK TV and radio stations can be picked up in Jersey and the majority of hotels now have satellite TV.

MONEY

English sterling is freely accepted on the island, as are UK cheques and all major debit and credit cards. Jersey issues its own banknotes (including a £1 note) and coins, and these can only be used in the Channel Islands. You will often be given change in Jersey currency, but UK banks will exchange Jersey notes (not coins) for sterling. You can also do this at the bank at Jersey airport, although a £30 limit is placed on changing cash amounts of Jersey currency to English sterling.

There are ATMs in St Helier, St Saviour, St Peter, Red Houses, the airport and harbour. For currency exchange banks offer a better rate than *bureaux de change*. A few shops accept euros.

O

OPENING HOURS

Banks. Banks have similar opening hours to those in the UK, with some open on Saturday morning.

Shops. Normal opening times are Mon–Sat 9am–5.30pm, but during summer a number of shops, particularly in St Helier, are also open in the evening. There is no general Sunday opening in Jersey but a few convenience food stores remain open. The markets and some shops are closed on Thursday afternoon.

Tourist Attractions. Most museums and tourist attractions are open from April to October, daily 9am or 10am–5pm, though the times are subject to change. Jersey Tourism *(see under Tourist Office below)* can provide a list of current opening hours, or you can telephone them to check times for specific sites.

Pubs. Most pubs are open Mon–Sat 9am–11pm, Sun 11am–11pm.

P

POLICE

In an emergency dial 999. Along with the regular police Jersey has a network of honorary police officers who don't wear uniform.

POST OFFICES

The main post office is in Broad Street, St Helier and is open Mon–Fri 8.30am–5pm, Sat 9am–2pm. There are around 20 sub-post offices throughout the island. The island Bailiwick of Jersey has its own postal system and issues its own Jersey stamps, available from post offices and some shops. These must be used on all mail. Unlike the UK, mail is not divided into first and second class, there is just the one class. Jersey stamps are much in demand by collectors worldwide. The main post office has a philatelic display and stamp sales.

PUBLIC TRANSPORT

Bus. Connex Transport Jersey Ltd (tel: 01534 877772, www.mybus.je) provides a comprehensive and reliable network of buses, all radiating from the new bus terminal at Liberation Station, St Helier. Bus timetables are available online or free from the bus station and Jersey Tourism. Explorer tickets, allowing unlimited travel during your stay, are available for one, three and five days or a Weekender (£6, £15, £22 and £10 respectively). Tickets are valid for consecutive day travel only. Summer services from mid-May until early October are far more frequent than those off season. Connex also operate the seasonal 'Island Explorer' service, which provides four routes linking more than 20 island attractions, beaches and places of special interest. The routes connect with the normal bus network and you can use both services with the same pass.

Bus timetables can be accessed through your WAP-enabled mobile phone. For details go to the Connex website *(see above)*. You can also text the bus stop code (shown beside the bus stop) to 66556 to find out the arrival time of the next bus.

Taxi. Taxi ranks are only to be found at the airport, the arrivals building at the harbour and in various locations in St Helier. Rates vary according to the time and the day. Extra charges are made for waiting time and luggage carried in the boot. If you need a taxi call Citicabs, tel: 01534 499999, Clarendon Dragons, tel: 01534 871111 or Island Cabs, tel: 01534 625625.

For a lift with a difference try LimoBikes (tel: 01534 853287, www.limobikes.jersey.com) who will pick you up on a Harley Davidson. Tours are also available.

Le Petit Train. The little tourist trains with on-board commentaries are fun for families. They operate daily from April to October, departing hourly from Liberation Square, St Helier. There are two routes: the Town and Maritime Tour, taking in the harbour area and St Helier waterfront, and the Promenade Tour, which goes all the way to St Aubin, skirting the bay. Jersey Cycle Tours and Jersey Funbikes are under the same family management, and you can combine the train trip with a cycle ride to Corbière from St Aubin along the old railway route (now a cycle path), then return to St Aubin for the train back to St Helier. For information visit www.littletrain.co.uk.

R

RELIGION

The established church in Jersey is the Church of England but Methodism has had a strong influence on many of the islanders since John Wesley preached here in 1787. Of the 29 Methodist chapels that existed here in the 19th century, 18 are still in use. There is also a notable Roman Catholic presence, with a total of eight churches. Jersey Tourism Centre *(see page 132)* publishes a leaflet with the times and places of services for various faiths and denominations.

T

TELEPHONE

The UK telephone code for Jersey is 01534. When dialling from outside the UK preface the code by 44 (for the UK) and omit the 0. STD codes for the UK from Jersey are the same as those used from the UK. Public call boxes take coins. As in the UK international calls can be dialled direct from any public phone.

Mobile Phones. Beware of high charges for making and receiving calls on a UK mobile. Prices are set by the relevant UK service provider and, as the UK networks do not extend to Jersey, these are usually costed as international calls. The three networks are Jersey Telecom, Airtel-Vodafone (also referred to as 23403), and Sure Mobile (Cable & Wireless). Visitors with mobiles will either be linked automatically to a network, or can select the network manually. Jersey Telecom (www.jerseytelecom.com/visitors) has the best coverage and offers a 3G service (so you can make video calls while you're on the beach). The network also extends to the other Channel Islands. Customers who are using their mobiles outside the UK for the first time may be barred from roaming and should contact their UK service provider.

Some pay as you go phones do not function in Jersey.

TIME ZONES

As in the rest of the UK, the Channel Islands are on Greenwich Mean Time (GMT), with clocks moving forward in late March, and reverting back in late October.

New York	**Jersey**	Paris	Jo'burg	Sydney	Auckland
7am	**noon**	1pm	2pm	11pm	1am

TOURIST INFORMATION

The Jersey Tourism Visitor Centre (tel: 01534 448800, www.jersey.com) is located in Liberation Place next to the bus station. The office has a wealth of information on the island and can also arrange accommodation. It is open all year: Jun–Sep Mon–Fri 8.30am–5.30pm, Sat 9am–5.30pm, Sun 9am–2.15pm; Apr, May and Oct Mon–Fri 8.30am–5.30pm, Sat and Sun 9am–1pm only, Nov–March Mon–Fri 8.30am–5.30pm, Sat 9am–1pm.

Brochures and books on Jersey can be requested from the tourist office on tel: 01534 448877. A free brochure pack includes Pure Jersey, a lively holiday and travel magazine, and the Stay Jersey accommodation guide featuring most of the hotels and guesthouses. These can also be downloaded online from the website. In addition, the monthly magazine *What's On*, which can be picked up at the airport or harbour on arrival, contains a complete listing of events, and has information on attractions, activities, sports and entertainment. The Visitor Map of Jersey, available from Jersey Tourism Visitor Centre, marks all the main attractions of the island, along with sporting facilities and cycle routes. It includes a useful map of St Helier showing accommodation and town attractions.

If you're intending to do a fair amount of sightseeing it's worth purchasing a Jersey Pass, an all-inclusive ticket to 15 of the island's leading attractions, including Durrell Wildlife, Mont Orgueil Castle, Jersey War Tunnels and La Mare Wine Estate. Passes are available for two, four and six consecutive days. You can pick one up at Jersey Tourism's Visitor Centre, other outlets around the island or book online (www.jerseypass.com) or tel: 01534 448877. Costs are £16 for 2 days, £45 for 4 days and £59 for a week.

TRAVELLERS WITH DISABILITIES

The Jersey Tourism website (www.jersey.com, then click on 'About Jersey') has a comprehensive section on facilities for travellers with disabilities, detailing accommodation, attractions, transport services, parking and equipment for hire. Jersey Tourism also produce the useful 'Guide to Jersey for the Disabled'. On-street parking and public car parks have designated areas for UK and European Blue Badge holders. A shopmobility service operates from St Helier's Sand Street Car Park from Mon–Sat 10am–4.30pm, also at Durrell Wildlife Conservation Trust and Jersey War Tunnels (information on www.shopmobility.org.je). The Radar National Key Scheme operates in Jersey, and toilets with radar locks can be found in main centres and at most beaches. Visitors are advised to bring their own key, but they are available for loan (£5 deposit required) from Jersey Tourism.

W

WEBSITES AND INTERNET CAFÉS

WiFi access is available at the airport, Jersey harbour lounge, Liberation bus station and some hotels and cafés. Most of the internet cafés are concentrated in St Helier. Free access is available if you are eating or drinking at The City Bar & Restaurant, 75–7 Halkett Place, open Mon–Sat 10am–11pm, or at the Café Bar at the Pomme D'Or Hotel, Liberation Square, open Mon–Sun 7am–11pm, which also has WiFi access. At Jersey Library, Halkett Place, £1 buys you 30 minutes' internet use.

Here are some popular websites:

www.jersey.com The official Jersey website is packed with information and should cover all your needs, from how to get there, where to stay and eat, to transport, sports, activities and events. It is easy to use and gives interesting background information as well as all the practical details. (Don't confuse it with the site that calls itself www.jerseytourism.com but has scant information on the island.)

www.thisisjersey.com For Jersey news, lifestyle, entertainment, weather forecast and six-day tide tables, this website draws its information from the daily *Jersey Evening Post*.

www.islandlife.org This is the community website serving the Channel Islands.

Y

YOUTH HOSTELS

The only youth hostel on the island, at Haut de la Garenne, St Martin, closed in 2008 when the building became the focus of investigation into historic child abuse. The hostel will not be returning to the building but the YHA (Youth Hostels' Assocation) are currently in talks with the States of Jersey to find an alternative site.

Recommended Hotels

Jersey Tourism publishes a comprehensive illustrated guide to accommodation available on the island, including hotels, guesthouses, self-catering and camping. You can order a copy by phone (tel: 01534 448888) or access the information online at www.jersey.com. Reservations can be made either directly with the hotel or through JerseyLink, the official accommodation booking service of Jersey Tourism. Prices plummet in winter and you can get some great rates for weekends, Christmas and Easter, especially at the up-market hotels.

Self-catering is limited on Jersey but Jersey Heritage (tel: 01534 633304, www.jerseyheritage.org) has recently restored several beautifully located historic forts and follies on the coast for holiday lets (see page 117).

Grading of accommodation is optional but most establishments are assessed by the AA or Visit Britain (to the same criteria). Hotels, guesthouses and self-catering are assigned one to five stars, campsites one to five pennants. The rating reflects the overall quality of the experience, including hospitality, service, cleanliness and comfort you can expect, ie it is not based merely on facilities.

The price bands below are a rough indication of what you can expect to pay in high season (July-August) for a double room with bathroom, including breakfast. Half-board rates usually offer better value than B&B rates.

££££	over £200
£££	160–200
££	120–160
£	under £120

ST HELIER

La Bonne Vie £ *Roseville Street, St Helier, tel: 01534 735955, www.labonnevie-guesthouse-jersey.com.* A flower-decked entrance, chocolates and home-made fudge greet you on arrival at this home-from-home B&B. The house was built for a wealthy merchant in the 1890s, and is located a few minutes' walk from the town centre, and just two minutes' from the beach where the Havre des Pas tidal pool guarantees bathing at all times. Guest rooms are individually furnished and all have their own bathrooms.

Club Hotel & Spa ££££ *Green Street, St Helier, tel: 01534 876500, www.theclubjersey.com.* Small and sophisticated, Jersey's newest luxury hotel offers offers eight suites, 38 luxury rooms (complete with Bang & Olufsen portable telephones, feather beds and Frette Egyptian linen), a stylish spa with salt pool, thermal and rasul treatments and relaxation room and the Michelin-starred Bohemia restaurant headed by celebrity chef, Shaun Rankin *(see page 108)*.

Elizabeth Castle Apartment (£1,000 a week in high season), *Elizabeth Castle, St Helier, tel: 01534 633304, www.jerseyheritage.org.* Self-caterers with a sense of adventure will enjoy staying at the famous fortress in St Aubin's Bay. This is a small apartment (sleeping 4–6), set on two floors in the old barrack block off the parade ground. The setting is an islet, and when the sightseers leave the castle in the early evening you have the whole place to yourselves. The castle is only accessible by foot at low tide, but during castle opening hours an amphibious ferry operates every half hour at all tides.

Eulah Country House £££ *Mont Cochon, St Helier, tel: 01534 626626, www.eulah.co.uk.* This classy Edwardian guesthouse has nine sumptuous and individually furnished rooms, a peaceful garden setting and fine views over St Aubin's Bay. The house is furnished with period antiques and paintings, but there's no shortage of modern comforts when it comes to the guest rooms with their king-size beds and luxury bathrooms. The upstairs lounge has lovely sea views and a fully stocked bar. 15–20 minutes' walk to St Helier, five to the beach.

Grand Jersey ££££ *The Esplanade, St Helier, tel: 01534 722301, www.grandjersey.com.* Following a £15-million overhaul, the Grand Jersey is looking swish and glamorous. You can sip vintage bubbles in the Champagne Lounge (with a choice of 100 champagnes and fine sea views), dine in the seductive Tassili restaurant, with its black backdrop, wind down or work out in the stylish new Elemis spa and pool, or watch movies in the island's only private cinema.

Merton Hotel ££ *Belvedere Hill, St Saviour, tel: 01534 724231, www.mertonhotel.com.* A children's paradise, the hotel is best known for the aquatic thrills of the Aquadome. This domed indoor pool has water slides, cascade fountains and spa pools. The latest attraction is the £1-million Flowrider artificial wave, the easy way to learn surfing and bodyboarding. Add to this the Kids' Zone, with supervised activities and fun events, Activity Teens club, fitness centre, live music and shows – and there's never a dull moment. Bedrooms are modern and functional, with good-value weekly rates.

Millbrook House £ *Rue de Trachy, Millbrook, tel: 01534 733036, www.millbrookhousehotel.com.* Those who love tranquillity and tradition will appreciate this country house, set in 10 acres (4 hectares) of private grounds. Service is discreet, public rooms are furnished with antiques and there is no entertainment to shatter the peace. Twenty of the 24 guest rooms have sea or garden views. No pool but golf enthusiasts can practice on the 5-hole pitch and putt course.

Royal Yacht £££ *The Weighbridge, St Helier, tel: 01534 720511, www.theroyalyacht.com.* This 1930s hotel underwent a £25-million makeover not long ago and now has a state-of-the-art spa, fully equipped gym, indoor pool, fashionable brasserie and four bars, including a live music venue and champagne bar. For the ultimate in luxury opt for a penthouse suite, with a jacuzzi on the harbour-view terrace and space for 10 guests to dine.

AROUND THE ISLAND

GOREY

The Moorings ££ *Gorey Pier, St Martin, tel: 01534 853633, www.themooringshotel.com.* In the heart of Gorey, this small hotel sits at the foot of the ancient castle of Mont Orgueil. Many of the 15 rooms have views over the picturesque harbour, where boats depart for trips to Normandy. The restaurant is well known for Jersey specialities, especially the seafood platter, which is also served in the Pier Bar & Bistro, which has a smaller, cheaper menu and a heated alfresco terrace overlooking the port.

ROZEL

Château La Chaire £££–££££ *Rozel Bay, St Martin, tel: 01534 863354, www.chateau-la-chaire.co.uk.* In a secluded spot at the foot of Rozel Valley, this traditional country house hotel has a rococo lounge with fine mouldings, an oak-panelled dining room, conservatory and 14 luxury rooms, some with spa bath and four-poster beds. Guests receive a warm welcome, and – included in the B&B room rate – a Jersey cream tea. Leave room for dinner though – the restaurant is noted for fine cuisine. The green valley stretches down to the delightful fishing creek of Rozel.

ST AUBIN

Cardington House ££££ *Mont es Tours, St Aubin, tel: 01534 748000, www.cardintonhouse.com.* Tucked away above the harbour this mid-19th-century mansion has recently been transformed from a private residence into an exclusive five-suite boutique hotel. A peaceful retreat, it has glorious bay views and immaculate gardens with steps leading down to a heated pool and hot tub. Contemporary style, sophisticated decor throughout. The 'Lord of the Manor' offer (from £1,000) gives you exclusive use of the house for a day and night, with accommodation for 10 guests.

Harbour View £ *St Aubin Harbour, tel: 01534 741585, www.harbourviewjersey.com.* Right in the centre of St Aubin, this creeper-clad guesthouse is set back from the road and picturesque harbour. Friendly, laid-back and family-run, it is one of Jersey's most popular guesthouses. There are 14 bedrooms, two suites and a welcoming garden terrace serving teas and light snacks. Guests can enjoy discounted early evening dinners at the highly rated Danny's Restaurant next door *(under separate ownership, see Restaurants page 112).*

Hotel Cristina £££ *Mont Felard, St Aubin's Bay, tel: 01534 758024, www.cristinajersey.co.uk.* Spectacular views of St Aubin's Bay are the main attraction of this recently refurbished hotel, and it's certainly worth paying the extra to secure a room with a south-facing balcony and sea view. Guests can dine at the Indigo restaurant, or lunch in the lounge bar, sun terrace or around the pool. The 63 guest rooms are well-equipped and furnished in light, contemporary style.

Old Court House Inn ££ *St Aubin Harbour, tel: 01534 746433, www.oldcourthousejersey.co*. This harbour-view hotel dates back to 1450 and in the 17th century the cellars were used to store the plunder of Jersey privateers. Guest rooms are individually furnished and include a two-bedroomed penthouse suite with a private sun terrace. Various eating areas include the cellar restaurant, floral courtyard to the rear and the deck over the harbour.

Peterborough House ££ *Rue du Croquet, St Aubin, tel: 01534 741568; www.jerseyisland.com/peterborough-house.html*. Built in 1690, this is a small B&B on a cobbled St Aubin street, a short walk from the colourful fishing harbour and its many restaurants. For a nominal supplement you can book a sea-view room. Public areas comprise two lounges, one with a bar and a sea-view terrace. No children under the age of 10.

ST BRELADE

Atlantic Hotel ££££ *Le Mont de la Pulente, St Brelade, tel: 01534 744101, www.theatlantichotel.com*. This small and desirable hotel, with dramatic views over the Atlantic, has been under local family ownership since it opened in 1970. It underwent a complete facelift for the Millennium and today's look is crisp, clean, light and contemporary. The striking sea-view Ocean restaurant, all in white, blue and beige, provides the backdrop for the Michelin-starred cuisine, based on local ingredients (*see Restaurants, page 112*). Facilities include the Palm Club with indoor pool, spa pool, mini-gym and saunas, and all-weather tennis court. The hotel backs on to La Moye Golf Club.

Les Ormes Self Catering, (£999–£1,599 per apartment per week) *Mont à la Brune, St Brelade, tel: 01534 497000; www.lesormes.je*. This popular self-catering complex comprises 24 cedar-clad lodges at Les Ormes near St Brelade's Bay and six coastal cottages at La

Pulente, overlooking St Ouen's Bay, with its great surf and stunning sunsets. On-site leisure facilities at Les Ormes include an indoor pool, gym, tennis, 9-hole golf course and the Creepy Valley Activity Centre *(see Activities, page 98).*

L'Horizon Hotel & Spa ££££ *St Brelade's Bay, tel: 01534 743101, www.handpicked.co.uk/lhorizon.* A house was originally built here in 1850 by a colonel in the Bengal Army – though he wouldn't recognise it now. L'Horizon has moved with the times. The interior is all space, light and elegance, the guest rooms contemporary in style with plasma TV screens, broadband and MP3 docking stations. But the views haven't changed. Sitting right on one of the island's finest beaches, the hotel enjoys glorious sea views. In the unlikely event that the sea doesn't tempt you there is always the indoor saltwater spa pool, which has sea views.

St Brelade's Bay Hotel ££££ *St Brelade's Bay, tel: 01534 746141, www.stbreladesbayhotel.com.* This comfortable, relaxing hotel, set in immaculate 7-acre (3-hectare) gardens and overlooking the best family beach on the island, is a winner. It has been in the same family for five generations, and the welcome is friendly. Public rooms are elegant with parquet floors, fine paintings and traditional furniture. Summer BBQ lunches are served at the Pool Bar and Grill. There is plenty to keep the whole family amused, from the play area, games room and sauna to croquet, a putting green and tennis court. The beach, just across the road, offers a wide range of water sports.

ST CLEMENTS

Shakespeare Coast Hotel £–££ *St Clements Coast Road, tel: 01534 851915, www.shakespearejersey.com.* This is the most southerly hotel in the British Isles, with (weather permitting) views to the coast of France. The restaurant offers good-value *table d'hôte* meals (especially if you are on half board), catering for vegetarians as well as meat and fish eaters. There are scooters and bikes to hire, a new games room and gym, and a beach across the road with free deckchairs for guests. St Helier is just 2 miles (3km) away, linked by the hotel minibus.

ST PETER

Boscobel Country Apartments (£699–£985 per apartment per week) *Rue Des Vignes, St Peter, tel: 01534 725259 or 01534 488141; www.boscobel.co.uk*. Seven purpose-built apartments on an old Jersey farm, surrounded by extensive pastureland. Traditional style, well-equipped accommodation, with satellite TV and high-speed broadband in every apartment.

Greenhills Country Hotel £££ *St Peter's Valley, St Peter, tel: 01534 481042, www.greenhillshotel.com*. A welcoming country house in the heart of St Peter's parish, Greenhills was converted from a late 17th-century home and still retains features from the original building. Decor throughout is traditional with wood panelling in the lounge, floral fabrics and antiques. The heated swimming pool is set in award-winning gardens, and meals are served alfresco in summer.

St Peter Country Apartments (£927–£1300 per apartment per week) *Mont Fallu, St Peter, tel: 01534 495495*. These are well-equipped apartments located a short drive from St Brelade's Bay or St Ouen's. Accommodation focuses around the heated outdoor pool and gardens. Rates include use of spa, gym and jacuzzi, and there is a children's play room, play area and a bar/café. Short breaks (minimum three days) are available in low or mid-season.

ST SAVIOUR

Longueville Manor ££££ *Longueville Road, St Saviour, tel: 01534 72550, www.longuevillemanor.com*. The most desirable country house hotel in the Channel Islands, this 14th-century manor is set in 15 acres (6 hectares) of fine gardens and woodland. No expense has been spared in the decor, with its elegant fabrics and fine antiques, and the service is impeccable. The restaurant may have lost its Michelin star but it is still renowned for cuisine – with vegetables fresh from the kitchen garden. To help work off the calories there is an all-weather tennis court and a heated outdoor pool.

INDEX

Berlitz pocket guide

Jersey

First Edition 2010

Written by Susie Boulton
Series Editor: Tony Halliday

Photography credits
All pictures by Anna Mockford and Nick
Bonnetti/Apa except page 20 by Mary Evans
Picture Library

Cover picture: Pictures Colour Library

Printed in Singapore by Insight Print
Services (Pte) Ltd, 38 Joo Koon Road,
Singapore 628990. Tel: (65) 6865-1600.
Fax: (65) 6861-6438

Berlitz Trademark Reg. U.S. Patent Office
and other countries. Marca Registrada

Every effort has been made to provide
accurate information in this publication,
but changes are inevitable. The publisher
cannot be responsible for any resulting
loss, inconvenience or injury.

Contact us

At Berlitz we strive to keep our guides as
accurate and up to date as possible, but if you
find anything that has changed, or if you have
any suggestions on ways to improve this guide,
then we would be delighted to hear from you.

Berlitz Publishing, PO Box 7910,
London SE1 1WE, England.
fax: (44) 20 7403 0290
email: berlitz@apaguide.co.uk
www.berlitzpublishing.com

Berlitz®
www.berlitzpublishing.com

BERLITZ PHRASE BOOKS
The Perfect Companion for your Pocket Guides

Speaking Your Language

Available in more than 30 languages, including Mandarin Chinese, Danish, Hindi and Hungarian